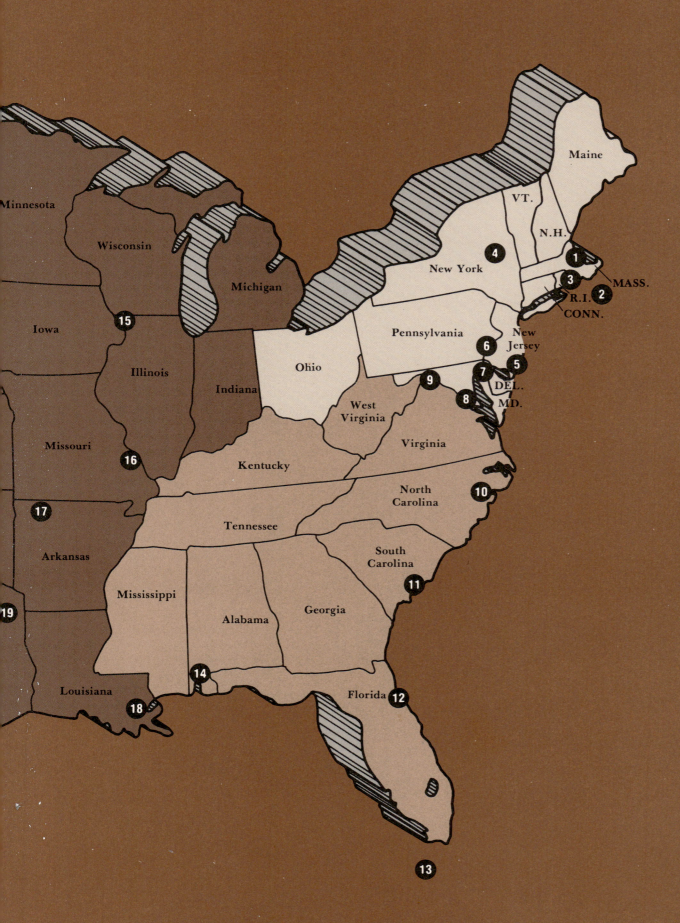

Historic Towns
OF AMERICA

The Northeast

1 Boston, Massachusetts
2 Nantucket, Massachusetts
3 Newport, Rhode Island
4 Saratoga Springs, New York
5 Cape May, New Jersey
6 Philadelphia, Pennsylvania
7 Annapolis, Maryland

The South

8 Georgetown, District of Columbia
9 Harpers Ferry, West Virginia
10 Bath, North Carolina
11 Charleston, South Carolina
12 St. Augustine, Florida
13 Key West, Florida
14 Mobile, Alabama

The Central States

15 Galena, Illinois
16 Ste. Genevieve, Missouri
17 Eureka Springs, Arkansas
18 New Orleans, Louisiana
19 Jefferson, Texas
20 Fredericksburg, Texas
21 Abilene, Kansas
22 Brownville, Nebraska

The West

23 Central City, Colorado
24 Silverton, Colorado
25 Helena, Montana
26 Taos, New Mexico
27 Salt Lake City, Utah
28 Austin, Nevada
29 Columbia, California
30 Monterey, California

HISTORIC TOWNS
OF AMERICA

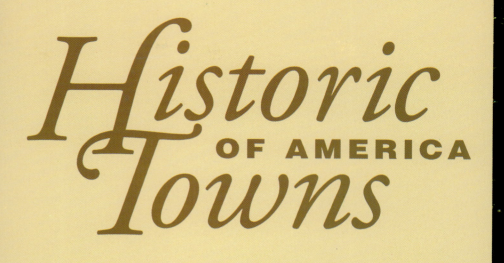

Historic
OF AMERICA
Towns

**PHOTOGRAPHS BY LYNN RADEKA
AND ALAN BRIERE**

TEXT BY GARY FISHGALL

MALLARD PRESS

**An imprint of BDD Promotional Book Company, Inc.,
666 Fifth Avenue, New York, New York 10103**

MALLARD PRESS

An imprint of BDD Promotional
Book Company, Inc.
666 Fifth Avenue
New York, N.Y. 10103

Mallard Press and the accompanying duck
logo are registered trademarks of the BBD
Promotional Book Company, Inc. Registered
in the U.S. Patent Office, Copyright © 1992

First published in the United States of
America in 1992 by The Mallard Press.

All Rights Reserved.

Copyright © 1992 by M & M Books

ISBN 0-7924-5656-4

AN M&M BOOK

Historic Towns of America was prepared and
produced by M & M Books, 11 W. 19th
Street, New York, New York 10011.

Project Director Gary Fishgall

Editorial Assistants Maxine Dormer, Ben
D'Amprisi, Jr.; *Copyediting and Proofreading*
Judith Rudnicki.

Designer Binns & Lubin/Martin Lubin and
Mariana Francis

Separations and Printing Regent Publishing
Services Ltd.

Previous pages:
p. 1: the Sea Mist Apartments, Cape May,
New Jersey
pp. 2–3: Cornhill Street, Annapolis,
Maryland
pp. 4–5: fireplace detail, Eureka Springs,
Arkansas
pp. 6–7: firehouse, Columbia, California
pp. 8–9: picket fence and tea plants, Key
West, Florida
pp. 10–11: the Chase–Lloyd House,
Annapolis, Maryland

These pages: Ft. Gaines at sunrise, Mobile,
Alabama

CONTENTS

INTRODUCTION

This is a book about cities, American cities. It may seem at first glance that this is a narrowly focused inquiry, concentrating on a single aspect of human endeavor, but even a cursory review of the contents of this book will suggest otherwise. For much of the history of the United States is to be found—albeit glancingly—within these pages. Indeed, as we travel together from the Northeast to the South, to the Midwest, and finally to the Pacific Coast, you will find that this is as much a journey through time as it is through space. Along the way, we will encounter the events that gave rise to the nation's earliest settlements; the conditions that led to the Revolutionary War; the young United States' emergence as a presence in international trade; the impact of the War of 1812 and the Mexican War; the increasingly bitter divisiveness between the North and the South which culminated in the Civil War; the great westward migration that extended the reach of the United States from coast to coast; and the fabulous glitter of the Gilded Age, when great fortunes were made and America grew up. Our traveling companions will include colonials seeking religious freedom, sea captains, mountain men, fur trappers, gunfighters, entrepreneurs, priests, prospectors, and even pirates and voodoo worshipers. But we will be joined as well by many ordinary men and women, people who simply wanted to build fruitful lives for themselves and their families in a bountiful new land.

Some of the places covered in this book are great metropolitan areas; others are sleepy backwaters. There are those with thriving commercial lives, and those that left their most productive years behind them long ago. By examining how each individual place emerged and developed, what economic base it fostered, and who its principal boosters were, we will hopefully come to appreciate how unique each American city is. It is easy in this age of rapid transport and mass communications, of fast-food restaurants and giant shopping malls with national chain stores, to visit a

place one has never been before and find it somehow familiar. But as Tom Palmer, the author of *Helena: The Town and the People*, put it, "Once you know what has happened in a place it feels different, [it] lends it character and personality."

It is true that the commonalities shared by today's cities tend to blur their differences, but each American town is, in fact, distinguished by its own own geography, history, and character. The places in this book simply emphasize their own unique qualities. That is because, despite their considerable differences, they share one overriding concern—the desire to preserve their architectural heritage. Visiting these places allows one to step back in time for a moment, to sample life in another age.

The preservation of old, often decaying structures in the face of ever advancing modernization is not easy and may often be a matter of chance. I am reminded of my first visit to Annapolis, Maryland, where I toured the magnificent home of signer of the Declaration of Independence William Paca. It was hard to imagine, as an engaging docent took me around the restored structure, that this splendid example of Georgian architecture had all but disappeared within the larger confines of a hotel and that it, along with the hostelry, was nearly lost to make room for a steel-and-glass office tower. As the preservation of the William Paca house tells us, there is often only the slightest circumstance—perhaps someone being in the right place at the right time or perhaps a visionary with incredible will power and tenacity—separating an historic structure's survival from its meeting with the wrecker's ball.

Despite their dedication to preserving their histories, the places in this book are not living history museums. Colonial Williamsburg, wonderful though it is, is not included here, for its costumed interpreters only pretend to inhabit the meticulously restored and re-created 18th-century community. They live in the 20th-century town that surrounds it. By contrast, the places in this book are all home to a group of people, from the 300 residents of Austin, Nevada to the millions who live in Boston and Philadelphia. All of the trappings of 20th-century life may be found in these places. They have simply been tailored to suit the ambience of another time.

This book marks the culmination of a series of volumes produced by Mallard

Books. Although this is the first that I have written myself, I have served as the project director and editor for the others. The direct antecedent was *Legendary Towns of the Old West*, published in 1990, with photographs by Lynn Radeka and text by John Bowen. In creating the present volume, Lynn again photographed the communities in the western half of the country and Alan Briere, who had done a splendid job with our book on Civil War battlefields, *Hallowed Ground*, joined us for the eastern half. To avoid repeating ourselves, Lynn and I chose new towns to replace those explored in the earlier book. The selection process unearthed some genuine finds, including Eureka Springs, Arkansas; Central City, Colorado; and Fredericksburg, Texas, but readers looking for the more familiar places—Dodge City, Kansas; Deadwood, South Dakota; and Lincoln, New Mexico, for example—are advised to consult the previous volume.

By way of conclusion, I would like to thank Lynn and Alan for their excellent work on this book and on the others we have done together. I would also like to thank: Maxine Dormer for her invaluable assistance on several aspects of the project; Ben D'Amprisi, Jr. for his help in computerizing the voluminous reference material gathered along the way; our designers, Martin Lubin and Mariana Francis of Binns & Lubin, for making the result so attractive; and Stephen Weitzen and Harold Clarke of BDD Promotional Books for their continuing support. Finally, I would be remiss if I didn't acknowledge the people in the towns we have covered and in other historic places as well who have worked so hard to preserve the treasures of the past. It is they who make America's historic towns fun and edifying to visit.

(Opposite) **The House of the Seasons, Jefferson, Texas.**

The Northeast

(*Above*) When Boston's population rose early in the 19th century, many of the town's wealthier citizens chose to settle on Beacon Hill, the once-insignificant pastureland near the newly completed State House. As the two homes pictured here suggest, the ambiance of the present Beacon Hill recalls those earlier times.

(*Opposite*) This is a closeup of the flag and rigging of the U.S.S. *Constitution*, berthed in the Charlestown Navy Yard. Nicknamed "Old Ironsides" for its solid oak construction, this frigate saw action in a number of battles during the War of 1812. Launched in 1797, it is the world's oldest commissioned warship still afloat.

(*Previous pages*) The grounds of the Elms, Newport, Rhode Island.

No city ever began with higher moral purpose. "We must delight in each other; make each other's condition our own; rejoice together, mourn together, labor and suffer together," wrote John Winthrop. He believed that his community would be "a City upon a Hill," a model for others to follow.

Winthrop was governor of the Massachusetts Bay Company, founded in 1629 by 12 Puritan gentlemen whose sect sought to live free of what they saw as the corrupting influences around them. Unlike the Pilgrims who had founded the Plymouth colony in 1624, the Puritans did not want to separate from the Anglican Church, but merely to reform it. The charter they acquired from a group of merchants—the King would never have granted them land of their own in America—gave their colony a measure of self-government that they considered imperative. Thus Massachusetts Bay's independent streak—which so plagued Mother England in later years—stemmed from the colony's very founding.

Arriving in the New World in the summer of 1630, Winthrop chose a site on a peninsula on what became known as the Charles River. By the middle of October, about 150 settlers were living in the community. They called it Boston, for the town in Lincolnshire, England, from which many of them hailed.

It didn't take long for the colonists to identify their greatest asset—the bay, which was deep enough to accommodate the largest of seagoing vessels and shallow enough along the coast to provide for the easy construction of wharves and piers. Soon enterprising merchants were building ships to carry goods to Europe and the Caribbean, and Boston had become the leading port in the colonies. The city was also the source of a wide variety of manufactured goods, including leather products, inexpensive furniture, and horse-drawn vehicles.

Problems between Boston and its mother country were not long in coming. After all, England's principal reason for establishing New World colonies was to acquire a source of

valuable raw materials. By turning to the sea rather than to agrarian enterprises, which the lands of New England could hardly support, the Bostonians had become competitors instead of suppliers. The so-called Navigation Acts, passed in 1660 and 1663, were designed to curb their efforts, forcing the colonists to refrain from trading with other nations when it came to highly prized commodities like tobacco, indigo, and cotton. In October 1684 England further tightened its grip by annulling the community's original charter and making Massachusetts Bay a royal colony.

Conditions improved somewhat during the rule of William and Mary, but the end of the French and Indian War in 1763 saw a re-emergence of tight British controls. Among other things, a special tax was placed on all legal and commercial documents. In response, Boston merchants instituted a boycott

Massachusetts Bay's first governor was John Winthrop, a prominent English attorney and country squire. Like the other Puritans who founded the colony with him, Winthrop sought to live free of what he saw as the corrupting influences around him.

Dominating this twilight view of the waterfront is Faneuil Hall, which wealthy merchant Peter Faneuil donated to the city in 1742. It is often called the "Cradle of Liberty" for the many anti-British assemblies that were held here prior to the Revolutionary War. Today the hall, with its many small food and gift stalls, is a popular gathering place for tourists.

of British goods while mobs of citizens attacked the homes of the king's representatives. Finally King George III, who had ascended the throne in 1760, repealed the tax, a decision that inspired one of the biggest celebrations in Boston's history.

Thereafter the city enjoyed two relatively quiet years, during which Boston's biggest concern was competition from rising seaports like Salem and Newport. Then, in 1767, new duties were levied on several key imported goods and the colonists again were inflamed. The protests in Boston—led by 46-year-old Samuel Adams—were so vocal that the governor dissolved the colony's legislative assembly and brought in additional troops to quell unrest. But matters got worse. On March 5, 1770, a group of redcoats fired on a band of citizens, killing five, in what became known as the Boston Massacre.

Again the hated duties were abolished—all of them, that is, except the one on tea. Consequently some 50 Bostonians, disguised as Indians, boarded the tea-bearing ships in their harbor on December 16, 1773, and tossed the hated cargo into the sea. Parliament, in turn, passed a bill that closed the city's harbor to all trade.

The Boston Port Bill crippled the town. Virtually all commerce—maritime or otherwise—ceased. Some residents left to find work elsewhere but those who remained persisted in their defiance of British authority.

The biggest showdown thus far came on April 18, 1775, when nearly 800 redcoats were dispatched to Concord, some 20 miles outside of Boston, to confiscate a cache of rebel military supplies. Several Bostonians, including the noted silversmith Paul Revere, rode swiftly through the countryside to alert local patriots—called Minutemen. At Lexington, some 70 armed citizens confronted the soldiers, shots were exchanged, and eight citizens were killed. A second skirmish occurred at Concord.

Two months later, on June 17, 1775, the first actual battle between the

THE BOSTON TEA PARTY
BOSTON HARBOR A TEAPOT TO-NIGHT! HURRA FOR GRIFFIN'S WHARF!

(Above) One of the most celebrated events in Boston history occurred on the night of December 16, 1773, when some 50 patriots disguised themselves as Indians, boarded the British tea-bearing ships in their harbor, and tossed the hated cargo overboard to protest against what they saw as taxation without representation.

(Right) The fiery abolitionist William Lloyd Garrison commenced publication of his newspaper, *The Liberator*, in January 1831, but he earned little praise from Boston mill owners and those dependent on them. They feared that his resolute stance against slavery would interfere with their southern sources of raw cotton.

British and Americans erupted at Breed's Hill in Charlestown, just across from the Boston peninsula. In this engagement, which history remembers as the Battle of Bunker Hill, the redcoats carried the field and Boston became an occupied enemy town.

When Gen. George Washington and his troops finally liberated the city on March 17, 1776, it was in very sorry shape. But the Bostonians set about rebuilding and in time their ships were not only vigorously prowling the Caribbean, they were sailing the Pacific, leading the way to highly profitable trade with China. With the rise in prosperity, the number of Bostonians grew to 30,000 by 1810, a fivefold

increase over the population during the British occupation.

While Boston's geography changed dramatically during the early years of the 19th century, enhanced by the Neoclassical architecture of Charles Bulfinch, the community's rigid class system remained largely intact. At the top of the social structure was an aristocracy composed of the town's old mercantile families and the founders of the area's new textile industry. These "Boston Brahmins," as writer Oliver Wendell Holmes called them, were powerful within their own province, but they were unable to extend their influence to the national scene. When, in 1812, most of them and indeed the

Built in 1712, the Old State House at Washington and State streets was the seat of the colonial government. The lion seen in closeup here is matched by a unicorn on the opposite side, the two creatures being the twin symbols of Great Britain. Today the Old State House is a museum of Boston history.

governor of the state opposed war with the British, they showed how clearly out of sync they were with prevailing sentiments elsewhere. Nonetheless Boston suffered along with the rest of New England during the conflict, as British ships blockaded the harbor, bringing the town's maritime activities to a virtual halt.

Eight years after the war's conclusion, on January 7, 1822, the town was officially incorporated and the first mayor—John Phillips—elected. In the ensuing decades, Boston became the center of tremendous intellectual and literary activity, sparked by such men and women of letters as Ralph Waldo Emerson, Henry David Thoreau, Nathaniel Hawthorne, Henry Wadsworth Longfellow, John Greenleaf Whittier, and Louisa May Alcott.

But no one stirred the city more than William Lloyd Garrison, who commenced publication of his newspaper, *The Liberator*, in January 1831. Many were infuriated with the fiery abolitionist for jeopardizing the precious relationship between the area's textile mills and their southern sources of raw cotton. A mob even attacked and nearly lynched him in 1835.

But by the 1840s and 1850s most Bostonians had come to find slavery intolerable. And when the Civil War

(*Left*) Adjacent to the Common and the edge of the historic district are the Public Gardens, the oldest botanical gardens in the country. Established in 1837, they owe their present configuration—with serpentine walks and flower beds—to the 1860 design of Boston landscape architect George F. Meacham.

Local folklore has it that charming Acorn Street on Beacon Hill was originally the home of servants and tradesmen. They worked for the wealthy families who lived on nearby Chestnut Street.

Completed in 1809, the Park Street Church became known as "Brimstone Corner" because gunpowder was stored here during the War of 1812. Fifteen years after the conclusion of the conflict, the fiery abolitionist William Lloyd Garrison delivered his first anti-slavery speech from this church.

Long before the movie *Glory*, the noted sculptor Augustus Saint-Gaudens celebrated the achievements of the Boston-based 54th Massachusetts Regiment, the first all-black unit in the Civil War, and their white commander, Robert Gould Shaw. This bronze relief stands on Boston Common across from the State House.

erupted, Boston was among the first cities to respond to President Lincoln's call for troops. Among the most notable of the city's regiments was the 54th Massachusetts, the first black unit raised by any state.

After the Civil War, Boston, which had been an industrial and financial leader in decades past, lost ground to other parts of the country, notably New York, where giants like Cornelius Vanderbilt established vast empires. "We are vanishing into provincial obscurity," lamented one prominent city booster. Nevertheless, the look and character of the city changed dramatically in the latter decades of the 19th century. Large parts of the peninsula's thin "neck" were filled in, establishing popular new residential districts such as the Back Bay. What had once been a town of some 780 acres had grown to an area nearly 30 times its original size. And by 1875, the population had reached 341,000.

Many of the newcomers were immigrants, including the Irish who had a difficult time establishing themselves in the largely Anglo-Saxon, Protestant city. By the turn of the century, however, sons of Eire like Patrick J. Kennedy and John F. ("Honey Fitz") Fitzgerald—the grandfathers of John F. Kennedy—controlled their own Democratic fiefdoms. Fitzgerald even became mayor in 1905. But, without doubt, the most successful Irish politician in Boston—and, indeed, the dominant political figure in the city's modern age—was the irrepressible James Michael Curley, who served four terms as Boston's chief executive beginning in 1914.

Today Boston is a progressive, ultrasophisticated city. But within the heart of this lively metropolis, a thick, well-traveled red line called the Freedom Trail leads to 16 significant historic sites. Among these are the home of Paul Revere; Faneuil Hall, the locus of numerous anti-British assemblies prior to the Revolutionary War; and Park Street Church, the elegant 1809 structure where William Lloyd Garrison delivered his first anti-slavery address.

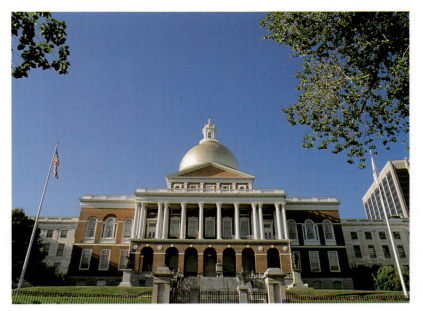

The Massachusetts State House, adjacent to the Boston Commons, stands on land once owned by the John Hancock family. Completed in 1798, it was the crowning work of the distinguished architect Charles Bulfinch, whose graceful Neoclassical structures virtually transformed the face of Boston in the 1790s and early 1800s.

The steeple in the background of this photograph belongs to the Old North Church, also known as Christ Church, built in 1723. It was from here that Paul Revere obtained the signal—"One if by land, two if by sea"—that told him of the British redcoats' route to Concord in 1775. In silhouette in the foreground is Cyrus E. Dallin's statue of the famous silversmith.

Without doubt, the most successful Irish politician in Boston—and, indeed, the dominant political figure in the city's modern age—was the irrepressible James Michael Curley, who served four terms as Boston's chief executive beginning in 1914.

(*Above*) Few resort communities offer the historic charm of Nantucket's Main Street, with its cobblestoned thoroughfare, absence of neon lights and fast food restaurants, and small stores in 19th-century structures.

(*Opposite*) This soaring clock tower belongs to the Unitarian Church. Although the main portion of the building dates from 1809, the tower itself was erected 24 years later. The bell is no longer in place.

Nantucketers have always been an independent lot. Even today, many of them refer to the mainland as the "United States," as if their tiny island 30 miles south of Cape Cod were a world unto itself.

Nantucket, meaning "the faraway land" in the language of the Indians who owned it, was acquired in 1659 by nine planters living north of Boston. The first Proprietors, as the new owners were called, sought to escape the oppressive atmosphere of the Puritan-dominated colony of Massachusetts Bay. By the following year, their community, which became known as Sherburne by 1673, encompassed some 60 settlers, including a carpenter, a shoemaker, and a miller-weaver. By 1720 the community's ranks had swollen to 721 and the small harbor where they had first settled had closed, so the settlers moved their town—houses and all—to its present harbor site, an area called Wesco, for a certain white rock located on what later became Straight Wharf.

During the town's early days, organized religion—which had played so pervasive a role elsewhere—was of little consequence. But the early years of the 18th century saw

(Above) Originally the shanties on the Old North Wharf were used by fishermen to sell their catches. Today most of these wooden structures have become residential cottages and are rented out to summer visitors.

(Right) Unable to support themselves as farmers, the Nantucketers turned to the sea, and in time, they became America's master whalers with a fleet of more than 80 ships.

Quakerism take root here, and by the start of the 19th century fully half the people on Nantucket were members of the Society of Friends.

At first, farming was the basis for the town's economy but the sandy lands of Nantucket were not suited to agriculture. The land wasn't conducive to ranching either; the sheep reared on the island were small and produced little wool. Clearly, another source of income had to be found and so Nantucketers turned to the sea.

The longstanding relationship between the island and the world's largest mammal began innocently enough. Some time after the establishment of the settlement, a right whale happened into the harbor and a group of villagers managed to kill it. Inspired by this episode, some began setting out in boats to look for whales in local waters. By the end of the century, the shore had been parceled into whaling territories, each equipped with a lookout station, where members of a six-man boating crew would take turns watching for their quarry. When a whale was spotted, the crew would hop in its boat and set out in pursuit.

Whereas the Indians had used the creatures for food, the colonists and their European counterparts prized the whale's baleen for ladies' corset stays and, above all, its blubber for lamp oil and candles. Particularly valued was spermaceti, from the oil in the head of the sperm whale, which was used chiefly for cosmetics and candles, for lustering linens, and in medicine as an emollient. By the early years of the 18th century, England alone was consuming more than 4,000 tons of whale oil annually.

In time, shore whaling gave way to forays on the high seas, and by mid-century Nantucketers were boldly setting forth on voyages that took them as far north as Greenland and as far south as Brazil. They had become America's master whalers with a fleet of more than 80 ships.

Among those who became wealthy from whaling was William Rotch, a Quaker who numbered among his crew a black slave named Prince Boston. When Rotch's ship docked in Nantucket in 1770, he gave each crew member—including Prince Boston—his rightful wages, but the slave's master objected, claiming the money belonged to him. Rotch, who did not believe in slavery, remained steadfast, taking the case to court and serving there as Prince Boston's advocate. When Rotch won, he struck the first blow for black emancipation in the Commonwealth; shortly thereafter the African-Americans of Nantucket were freed.

By the time of the American Revolution, there were some 5,000 people living on Nantucket. Those who were not directly involved in whaling were

This Main Street building stands on the site of a 19th-century structure that was damaged in a succession of fires, the most recent of which was in 1979. Thereafter the structure was rebuilt on the original foundation. The ship's model hanging over the door is the work of a local craftsman, Charles Sayle.

(Above) Old North Cemetery, shown here, features gravestones that date from the 18th century.

(Left) The celebrated Brant Point Lighthouse was built in 1901, but a ship's beacon has guarded the entrance to the Great Harbor from the same spot since 1746.

Among those who grew wealthy from whaling was William Rotch, a Quaker who became an advocate for black emancipation when he insisted upon paying a slave on his crew as he would have paid any other whaler.

most likely engaged in a related endeavor. The town soon boasted five wharves, rope walks, sail lofts, shipyards, and 36 factories where whale oil was converted into candles.

Unlike many on the Massachusetts mainland, few islanders sought independence from Great Britain. Indeed, Nantucket had enjoyed a rather special relationship with the mother country. Thus, when war came, the islanders sought to remain neutral. As a consequence, they fell prey to the forces of Britain *and* America. Their whalers were unable to roam the seas and the economy of the town collapsed. As the local agricultural output could only support about 10 percent of the population, many people starved, and, with virtually no timber to be had, others suffered from exposure during the cold New England winters. By 1783, when the combatants permitted Nantucket to take to the seas again, the town had lost nearly one-fifth of its population and the vast majority of its fleet had either been sunk or captured.

It took time but eventually the town rebounded. Then came the War of 1812, and Nantucketers faced many of the same kinds of privation that they had endured during the Revolutionary War. Again, after the war, the intrepid sailors began anew.

Meanwhile, the town continued to grow, numbering more than 7,000 resi-

The older of the two existing financial institutions on Nantucket Island is the Pacific National Bank, founded in 1804. Its impressive Federal-style headquarters, pictured here, was built in 1818.

dents by 1820. The following year even saw the founding of a local newspaper, the *Inquirer*. As the fortunes of the shipowners rose, they erected impressive mansions. Among the more notable achievements were the "Three Bricks," a trio of Neoclassical houses built by Joseph Starbuck for his sons for the then-staggering sum of more than $40,000. Across the street, William Hadwen erected the equally imposing "Two Greeks," one of which had a domed roof that opened to the stars. Not to be outdone, Jared Coffin commissioned an even finer house, one of the only three-story structures in town. These homes have survived to the present day, but much of the rest of Nantucket—some 400 buildings in total—was lost in a fire that began on July 13, 1846.

By the time of the great conflagration and the town's subsequent rebuilding, the island's whaling industry had reached its peak, with 88 locally owned vessels on the high seas. Even Herman Melville celebrated the Nantucketers' accomplishments, calling them "sea hermits" who "conquered the watery world like so many Alexanders."

Although the rewards of whaling were great, so were the perils. Consider the case of the *Essex*, which undertook its fifth voyage in 1818. Struck by a

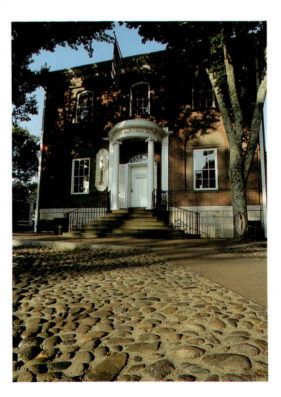

whale on the high seas, the ship capsized, leaving a crew of 20 struggling to survive in three boats with their target destination an estimated two-month voyage away. Eventually, the men resorted to cannibalism and, when their numbers weren't dying fast enough to feed the survivors, they drew lots to see who would be murdered.

Ironically, the boom in the whaling industry carried the seeds of Nantucket's eventual demise for, as the voyages took ships farther and farther afield and covered longer and longer periods of time—up to four years—larger and heavier vessels were needed. A sand bar across the mouth of Nantucket's harbor barred entry to these massive ships. To counter this problem, many of the island's whaling ships were outfitted and off-loaded on nearby Martha's Vineyard. In other instances, small boats would meet the heavily laden vessels outside of the port and relieve them of their cargoes. But this solution was time- consuming and rendered waiting ships vulnerable to sudden storms. In addition, voyages were becoming less profitable. Newcomers to the industry—foreign powers and such local ports as New Bedford, New London, and Sag Harbor—crowded the field, diminishing the supply of whales. The final blow came in 1854, when the first commercial production of kerosene brought a cheaper source of illumination to the marketplace.

The collapse of the whaling industry devastated Nantucket. From a high of 10,000 residents in the 1840s, the population plummeted to 3,201 by 1875. The island's rebirth began in the 1870s, when the Massachusetts Old Colony railroad decided that its future lay in promoting Nantucket, Martha's Vineyard, and Cape Cod as vacation sites. Their scheme worked and by the 1890s Nantucket had become one of the nation's premiere resorts. It continues to be so today. But it is a resort with a difference, for, amid the T-shirt shops and seafood stalls, there are pervasive reminders of Nantucket's rich historic past. There is Main Street, still cobble-

(*Above*) Now a renowned inn, the Jared Coffin House at 29 Broad Street was begun in 1845 for a wealthy shipowner and his family. At one time, the Greek Revival mansion was the only three-story structure on the island.

(*Right*) Built in 1686, the Jethro Coffin House is considered the oldest extant dwelling on Nantucket Island. Its design typifies that of a 17th-century home in the colony of Massachusetts Bay.

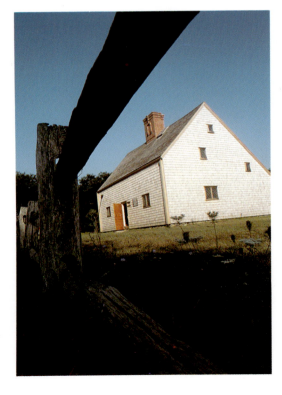

stoned. There is an impressive Whaling Museum, housed in an 1846 candle factory where whale oil was once processed. There is a working windmill and one of the most famous lighthouses in America. And, of course, there are the people, those who live on the island year-round. They're just as independent today as their ancestors were when they settled the "faraway land" more than 330 years ago.

(*Above*) The first Great Point Lighthouse, built by the federal government in 1785, burned down 31 years later, and the rubble-stone structure that replaced it toppled into the sea during a violent storm in 1984. But two years later, a replica, pictured here, was built with funds appropriated by Congress. It was set on a different site.

(*Above*) A cluster of buildings in wood and brick surround Washington Square, known formally as the Parade. It was here in the colonial age that troops trained and town meetings were held. The steeple rising in the distance belongs to City Hall. It is a replacement; the top floor of the structure burned in 1918.

(*Opposite*) Built in 1673, the White Horse Tavern at the corner of Marlborough and Farewell streets is considered the oldest tavern building in America. It continues to serve as a restaurant.

To quote a French observer from the 1890s, "On the floors of the halls, which are too high, there are too many Persian and Oriental rugs. There are too many tapestries, too many paintings on the walls of the drawing room; on the lunch and dinner tables, there are too many flowers, too many plants, too much silver, too much crystal."

Sociologist Thorstein Veblin called it "conspicuous consumption," and most would concede that the summer colony's villas evoking medieval castles and the palaces of Louis XIV were excessive, especially when one remembered that they were occupied for, at best, two or three months a year. But there was no denying their grandeur, nor that they and their glittering occupants had made Newport, Rhode Island the very quintessence of the Gilded Age.

In 1639, long before the town on Aquidneck Island in Narragansett Bay became a playground of the rich, it was settled by a group of Bostonians, led by merchant William Coddington. Seeking freedom from the strictures of the Massachusetts Bay colony, they made the community they

called Newport an exemplar of religious tolerance. "All men may walk as their consciences persuade them, everyone in the name of his God," stated the Code of Laws. This spirit of openness soon drew members of the Society of Friends, better known as Quakers, and followers of Judaism. It was in Newport in 1763 that the latter established Touro Synagogue, the first Jewish house of worship in North America.

The land around Newport was fertile and those who established farms there prospered. In addition, the town boasted an excellent natural harbor. By as early as the mid-17th century, local merchant ships were establishing trade with other New England seaports, occasionally venturing into New Amsterdam and by the 1680s reaching as far as the West Indies. They began by marketing local crops and dairy products, but such exports were in limited supply, owing to the relatively small size of the island. Other commodities had to be found. The most lucrative alternative was the slave trade, which the British had opened to private enterprise in 1689. By 1760 Newport dominated the unsavory business with no fewer than 180 slave ships on the open seas. Typically they would buy molasses in the West Indies, turn it into rum in Newport, where there were 22 distilleries by the middle of the 18th century, and exchange the rum for slaves in Africa. Crammed into ships' holds, the human cargo would then be transported to the West Indies for sale. The cash was used to buy more molasses, and the cycle—molasses to rum to slaves, appropriately known as the Triangle Trade—would begin all over again.

The Trinity Church in Queen Anne Square dates from 1725/26. Its interior includes the only three-tiered, wine-glass pulpit in America and an organ that was tested by Handel before it was shipped from England. Worshipers over the years have ranged from George Washington to Queen Elizabeth II.

As Newport's mercantile economy grew, so did the city. By 1730, the population had risen to 4,650, and the harbor was dotted with ships. Houses, still relatively close to the waterfront, stretched for several blocks inland, and beyond them lay the fields and homes of the area's farmers. In 1743, feeling somewhat alienated from the urban center that Newport had become, the latter won the right to form their own community, which they called Middletown.

Newport was not only growing in size, it was becoming quite cosmopolitan. In addition to people of various religions, the area's pleasant summer weather attracted wealthy plantation owners from the southern colonies and the West Indies, eager to escape the oppressive heat and the risk of malaria in their own backyards. The city's sophistication could be seen in the finery of its ladies and gentlemen and the skill of its craftsmen. Particularly

Still in use today, Touro Synagogue is the oldest Jewish house of worship in North America. The Georgian style structure was designed by British-born merchant Peter Harrison, who served as early Newport's amateur architect, and was dedicated in 1763.

(Top) At one time Mill Street, pictured here, was the site of an old stone mill. The Wist-Hathaway House is on the left in this photo.

(Above) Church Street was developed during the colonial period as part of Newport's downtown area. It was named for Trinity Church, which was—and is—located at a corner of one of the thoroughfare's principal intersections.

(Above) The society ladies pictured here are enjoying the swings at Bailey's Beach, the elite place in Newport for water enthusiasts.

(Right) The Chinese Teahouse on the grounds of Marble House was built in 1913 by Alva Vanderbilt, who had again taken up residence in the mansion in 1908, following the death of her second husband, Oliver Hazard Perry Belmont. During the years of their marriage, she had summered at Belcourt Castle across the street.

(Above) The first of Newport's luxury palaces was Marble House, a gift from William K. Vanderbilt to his wife Alva (right). Designed by the Vanderbilts' favorite architect, Richard Morris Hunt, this "cottage" featured 500,000 cubic feet of white marble and cost a staggering $11 million.

(Above) Perhaps because they lacked an ocean view, Julia and Edward Berwind lavished particular attention on the grounds of their summer estate, the Elms. They spent more than $300,000 on outbuildings and landscaping and employed a staff of 12 gardeners.

notable among the latter were Job Townsend and John Goddard, Quakers who became celebrated furniture-makers in the 1760s.

Perhaps the wealthiest of Newport's merchants was Godfrey Malbone, whose mansion was said to be the grandest home in America. Among its lesser known feautures was a tunnel that ran from the cellar to a secluded cove, through which Malbone could import goods without paying duties on them. Such "initiative" was not uncommon among the local merchants.

Despite their prosperity, the citizens of Newport were still dependent upon Boston for trade with London. That changed in the 1750s, however, when the population reached more than 6,000 and the community was large enough to support direct, sustained trade with the mother country. Freed at last from the Boston middlemen, Newport became a mercantile center of the first order.

Although most of the locals were loyal to Britain during its escalating differences with the colonies, the Revolutionary War brought disaster upon the Rhode Islanders. Ships of the Royal Navy began gathering in the harbor in spring 1775, leading many residents to flee the city and bringing commerce to a virtual halt. Finally, on December 7, 1776, some 8,000 redcoats occupied the town. They remained for three full years, and when they finally departed, a third of Newport's houses lay in ruins, the wood having been used for fuel. Some of those who fled the British invaders returned, but many did not. In 1782, the city's population was still little more than half its prewar total.

The war forever ended Newport's role as a major seaport. When the town blossomed again half a century later, prosperity came not from agriculture nor even from the sea, but from pleasure-seekers.

After the first vacationers arrived early in the 18th century, the numbers of Newport's summer visitors continued to accelerate. In the mid-1820s the town's first hotel was erected, and others soon followed. During the decades before the Civil War, most vacationers took up residence at one of these hostelries. An exception was George Noble Jones, a Georgia plantation owner who in 1841 built a charming Gothic Revival cottage that he called Kingscote. Eleven years later a China Trade merchant from New York named William S. Wetmore erected an even more imposing structure, an Italianate stone villa called Château-sur-Mer. At the time, these summer places may well have been the exceptions, but they were portents of things to come.

With the onset of the Civil War in 1861, the influx of vacationing Southerners ceased. Instead, the conflict brought to Newport the U.S. Naval Academy, whose home in Annapolis, Maryland was beset with Confederate sympathizers. The midshipmen found themselves ensconced at the Atlantic House, one of Newport's largest hotels, for the duration.

In the years immediately following the war, the summer business flourished once more, with six hotels serving vacationers by the end of the 1860s, along with a number of inns and lodges. The grandest of the hostelries was the Ocean House, a resort complex boasting some 600 beds and an excellent restaurant.

The 1870s and 1880s saw the emergence of a new American elite, captains of industry whose wealth and power exceeded anything that America had ever known before—or would ever know again. Fueled by fortunes made in transportation, real estate, manufacturing, and the stock market, the Vanderbilts, Astors, and other members of what Ward McAllister called the "400" ushered in a period of unparalleled extravagance. And Newport became their summer capital.

Not content to reside at hotels, they built residences of their own. Located primarily on prestigious Bellevue Avenue, these fantastic showpieces featured marble, gilt, rare woods, and molded plaster with meticulously manicured gardens and antique furnishings from England and France.

One of the first of the luxury palaces was Marble House, a gift from William K. Vanderbilt to his wife Alva. Designed by the Vanderbilts' favorite architect, Richard Morris Hunt, and featuring 500,000 cubic feet of white marble, this "cottage" cost a staggering $11 million. But no matter. It helped Alva Vanderbilt eclipse Mrs. William B. Astor as the leader of Newport's social set. Completed in 1892, Marble House was supplanted three years later by an even grander structure, the Breakers, built by William Vanderbilt's elder brother, Cornelius.

For the elite, summers in Newport meant a seemingly endless round of balls, dinner parties, and other social affairs, with a hostess spending $75,000 or more on a single event. The gentlemen entertained themselves at polo and yachting. There were clubs—the genteel Newport Reading Room, founded in 1853, and the upstart Casino, which played host in 1881, a year after its founding, to the first championships of the United States Tennis Association. Those who liked to swim could be found at Bailey's Beach, the elite place for water enthusiasts, while golfers took to the Newport Golf Club, established in 1893.

Designated a National Recreation Trail in 1975, the Cliff Walk, seen here at moonrise, follows the coastline starting at Memorial Boulevard. It carries intrepid rock climbers past a number of the resort's Gilded Age mansions.

The high point of each day's activities came with the afternoon carriage parade along Bellevue Avenue, a *de rigueur* event for the social elite.

This glittering way of life began to fade during the early years of the 20th century, when the trust-busting fervor of Teddy Roosevelt and the creation of a personal income tax in 1913 made it impossible for even the super rich to maintain their extravagant lifestyles. The advent of the First World War in August 1914 finished off the Gilded Age. In 1933, when Marble House was sold, it commanded only $100,000, less than one percent of what it had cost to build.

Today the town remains a popular summer resort. It also keeps a number of these breath-taking mansions open to the public, including six, among them Château-sur-Mer, Marble House, and the Breakers, that are maintained by the Preservation Society of Newport

County. In the heart of town, one will find what is purported to be the largest collection of 17th- and 18th-century structures in America, 85 of which were restored at a cost of about $15 million by a foundation established by Doris Duke in 1968.

(Above) Built in 1901 for Pennsylvania coal magnate Edward J. Berwind and his wife Julia, the Elms was modeled after a chateau near Paris by Philadelphia architect Horace Trumbauer. The chandelier that can be seen in this photo was powered, along with the other fixtures in the house, by a generator that Berwind installed on the grounds, there being no electricity in general use in the neighborhood.

(Left) For the Newport elite, the high point of each day's activities came with the afternoon carriage parade along Bellevue Avenue, a *de rigueur* event.

(Above) This Italianate Villa style structure on Circular Drive (right) was first home to attorney Augustus W. Shepherd in 1878. Thereafter until 1902 the house was occupied by other members of the Shepherd family. From 1944 to 1960 it served as a convent.

(Opposite) By 1909, most of Saratoga's fabled springs were exhausted, and New York State created a preserve to protect those that remained. In the 1930s, the Saratoga Spa State Park opened with a research laboratory, medical facilities, and three bathhouses, two of which, Lincoln bathhouse and Roosevelt bathhouse, are still operational today.

"Saratoga is all things to all men," someone once wrote. "It is a miniature world in itself; and here you may be grave or gay, wise or foolish, giddy or devout, as the mood seizes you." In its heyday the "miniature world" drew some 50,000 visitors a year. It was a glittering showplace, the epitome of the Gilded Age, and only Newport, Rhode Island could rival it for the honor of being America's premiere playground.

In the mid-1760s, long before the hotels and casinos came, the valley near the foothills of the Adirondack Mountains began attracting settlers. Called by the Indians Sarachtogoe, from *saragh*, Iroquois for "swift water," and *oga* meaning "place of," the name would later be Anglicized as Saratoga. By this time Native Americans had been visiting what they called the Medicine Springs of the Great Spirit for about 300 years, but few white men had seen it. Finally in 1771 Sir William Johnson, the British Superintendent of Indian Affairs in North America, was brought to the site.

Johnson had first visited the valley 33 years previously. A fair trader, he soon won the respect of the Mohawk Indians, who adopted him into the tribe. Perhaps it was the memory of the tall, vigorous Irishman in his prime that

(*Below*) The most famous of Saratoga's 20-plus springs was Congress Springs, discovered around the turn of the 19th century by a U.S. senator. It attracted throngs of visitors, in part because of the Greek portico in which it was enclosed by owner John Clarke. As seen in the 1880 photo at right, the shady pavilion afforded health-seekers a pleasant place in which to chat as they sipped glasses of the mineral water.

(*Below*) Among the first white men to view the healing springs that would eventually give rise to the Queen of Spas was Sir William Johnson, the British Superintendent of Indian Affairs in North America. Unable to walk, he was transported to the site in 1771 by his Mohawk friends.

moved the Indians in 1771, when they found him suffering from a variety of illnesses, unable to sit or stand, and transported him to the healing springs on a litter. Johnson partook of the salty waters for four days, but unfortunately, they seemed to do little to improve his condition.

For a decade after Johnson's encounter with High Rock Springs, as the whites came to call it, the village remained relatively small and isolated. Then, in the fall of 1777, the Revolutionary War came to the valley in the form of 7,000 redcoats under the British *bon vivant*, Maj. Gen. John Burgoyne. It fell to Maj. Gen. Horatio Gates, ably assisted by Benedict Arnold, to stop the man known as Gentleman Johnny. And stop him they did—at a battle about nine miles outside of Saratoga Springs on September 19, 1777. A second engagement on October 7 was even more successful. Finally, on October 17, the badly outnumbered British surrendered, giving the Americans their first victory of the war and encouraging the French to ally themselves with the struggling republic.

In the years after the war, stories of the spring's curative powers, repeated by the likes of George Washington, focused considerable attention on the area. Physicians published treatises on the waters, and lecturers and writers related wondrous tales in public forums. Finally in 1787 tavernkeeper Alexander Bryan built a rather tawdry public house near High Rock Spring. A much more imposing hostelry, the Union Hall, was completed in 1803 by Gideon Putnam. The frame structure, 70 feet long and three stories high, was located near Congress Spring, which had been discovered a short time earlier by a U.S. congressman, Nicholas Gilman.

Despite the difficulties of reaching the village, the Union Hall was an enormous success, and two years later Putnam expanded his hotel to twice its original size. In 1811 the innkeeper started an even more lavish place,

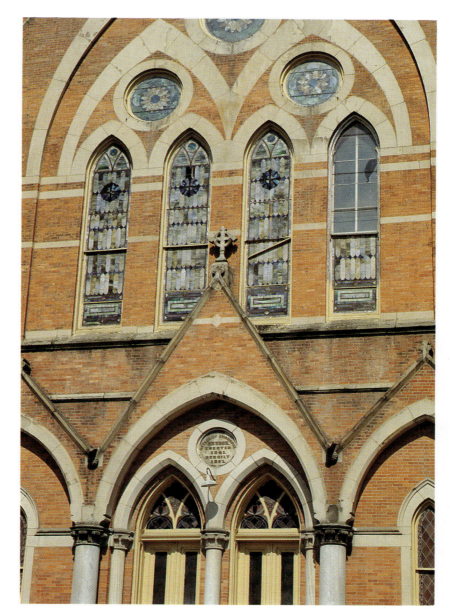

(Left) The Universal Baptist Church on Washington Street was built in 1870. It reflects the Gothic Revival style, although elements of the Renaissance Revival style can be seen in the right tower.

(Below) In the Gilded Age, as now, the highlight of the Saratoga season was the month of August, when the horses ran at the fabled Saratoga Race Track. The track was inaugurated in 1863 and has played host ever since to two classics of the sport of kings, the Travers Stakes and the Saratoga Cup.

(Opposite page) Strolling through Congress Park today, one sees curving walks, large shady trees, carefully groomed flower beds, and decorative elements, such as the two urns pictured here. These features evoke a bygone age when ladies and gentlemen promenaded through the grounds in their finery, seeing and being seen. The park was acquired by the city in 1911.

(Below) Broadway star Lillian Russell frequented Saratoga Springs during the Gilded Age. She was most often seen in the company of railroad equipment salesman extraordinaire Diamond Jim Brady, who once gave her a gem-encrusted bicycle.

which was completed after his death the following year by his wife and children, who named it Congress Hall.

Saratoga was indeed popular, but it offered visitors few entertainments. The moralizing posture of the community—which the locals deemed appropriate in a place of healing—didn't help. Finally in 1819 the civic leaders broke away from the town of Saratoga, creating an independent community which they called Sarataga Springs. Free to make their own regulations, they relented against such activities as gambling and dancing. The following year a billiard parlor opened in Congress Hall and an orchestra was engaged for evening entertainments. There were even balls.

In 1823 the land that included Congress Spring was purchased by Dr. John Clarke, one of the first soda fountain operators in America. Intending to retire on his new estate, Clarke instead found himself bottling waters from the springs and selling them all over the United States. It was the outset of the patent medicine craze, and the recognition that came to the spa through Clarke's entrepreneurship drew even more visitors. Not lacking in showmanship, the good doctor (whose title was

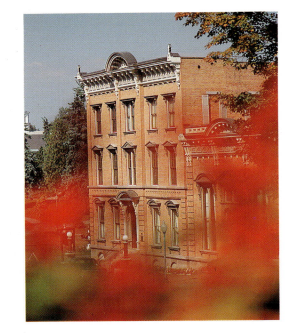

A Saratoga landmark for any sporting man of the Gilded Age was the Casino adjacent to Congress Park. Originally built by former heavyweight champ John Morrisey, who called it the Club House, the gaming parlor was later acquired by Richard Canfield, who renamed it and extensively refurbished it. Today it is a museum.

purely honorary) enclosed Congress Springs in an imposing Doric pavilion, built new, flower-strewn paths leading up to it, and arranged for bands to entertain visitors at the site each morning and afternoon.

Then on July 3, 1833, the railroad reached Saratoga Springs and the "Queen of Spas" experienced a tremendous boom, the number of visitors increasing from 6,000 to 8,000 in one year alone. Perhaps the resort's biggest attraction was the chance it offered average folks to mingle with the nation's social elite. "Hundreds who, in their towns, could not find admittance into fashionable circles of society," wrote one social observer, "come to Saratoga where . . . they may be seated at the same table, and often side-by-side, with the first families of the coun-

(Left) Designed by noted sculptor Daniel Chester French, the Spirit of Life Fountain in Congress Park is dedicated to Spencer Trask, a New York financier and a strong Saratoga booster. When he and his wife died, they left Yaddo, their large estate on the edge of town, as a retreat for artists and authors.

This French Renaissance style home on North Broadway originally belonged to Frank Wheeler, a ticket agent for the New York railroad. Over the years its occupants have included a Methodist minister, a lawyer, and a patternmaker. Today the house is broken up into a series of apartments.

try. . . ." This democratic spirit continued into the Gilded Age, when, by contrast, the elite summering at Newport, Rhode Island barricaded themselves within sumptuous private villas.

Although the struggle between the North and the South caused Saratoga to lose its many southern guests, the Civil War barely dented the tourist trade. Among those who arrived in 1861 was the former heavyweight boxing champion, John Morrisey. Nicknamed Old Smoke, the savvy but unrefined enforcer for New York's political machine, Tammany Hall, brought with him an array of roulette wheels, faro boxes, and other gaming equipment and opened a casino in town. Despite his crude ways, Morrisey was a model of decorum who generously endowed Saratoga charities; soon he and his casino were integral parts of the resort community.

Morrisey also built Horse Haven, a race track that opened on August 3, 1863, with a four-day program. The event was such a success that the following year saw the establishment of a larger and more impressive track across the street. Before long, as many as 10,000 people a day were attending the races at Saratoga.

In 1870, Morrisey opened up a new, very grand casino in the park surrounding Congress Spring. Among those who patronized the Club House—as the establishment was called—was Cornelius Vanderbilt, perhaps the richest man in America at the time.

After Old Smoke died in May 1878, the Club House was acquired by Spencer and Reed and later, in 1894, by Richard Canfield, who refurbished it and renamed it the Casino. The Prince of Gamblers insisted that his guests dress in evening clothes and hired a famous French chef to create culinary masterpieces for their pleasure. The restaurant lost a fortune each year, but Canfield's profits from the games of chance more than made up for the expense. One of his gentlemen customers, William Collins Whitney, for example, lost $385,000 in a single evening.

A third entrepreneur who played a prominent role in the spa's post-Civil War history was Alexander Stewart, the owner of Wanamaker's, then the largest department store in the world. In 1872, the king of retailers acquired the Grand Union Hotel and spent half a million dollars turning *it* into one of the world's largest hostelries. A new hotel, the United States, also opened in 1874 at a cost of about $1 million. Located on the site of a hotel of the same name that had burned down 50 years earlier, the new United States boasted an imposing, 30-foot-wide veranda that overlooked Broadway, the town's main street.

With hotels like the Grand Union and the United States and gaming houses like the Casino, Saratoga was one of the brightest lights of the Gilded Age. Tycoons, politicians, entertainers, social leaders, writers, and others of the nation's elite paraded across the town's carefully manicured parks and walkways, ate like royalty, lost fortunes at the track and the gaming tables, and sported the latest fashions, which the ladies transported in a seemingly bottomless piece of luggage with a curved top called—appropriately—a Saratoga Trunk.

Possibly no one epitomized the age better than a young elegant socialite named Evander Berry Wall, who on a memorable day in 1888 managed to make 40 complete wardrobe changes between breakfast and dinner for the sheer sport of it. But perhaps the pair most associated with the resort's heyday were the railroad equipment salesman extraordinaire, Diamond Jim Brady, and the toast of the Great White Way, Lillian Russell. Brady, a man of enormous appetites in every way, possessed, among other baubles, a different set of jewels for each day of the month. These included more than 20,000 diamonds. He once gave Russell a bicycle said to be gold-plated, with her initials in gems on the handlebars.

Today the Gilded Age is a memory, done in long ago by, among other things, the personal income tax and the advent of World War I. Most of Saratoga's fabled springs—57 were eventually found—were exhausted even before the great era of conspicuous consumption came to an end. Those that remain were acquired in 1909 by the State of New York, which has preserved them. Nevertheless the ghosts of the grand old days linger at Canfield's Casino, which now houses a museum; the Adelphi Hotel, which hints at the splendor of the other, long-gone hostelries of the Victorian Age; the hundreds of privately owned 19th-century homes; and, of course, the race track, where for a brief time each August the gamesters and social elite reconvene, reminding everyone of the glittering resort that once was Saratoga Springs.

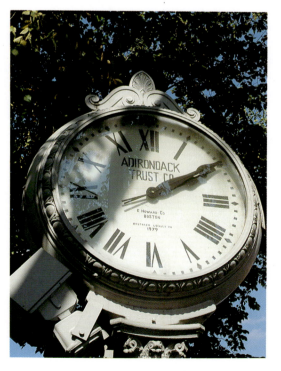

(*Above*) Saratoga National Historic Park, a short distance from the town, preserves the site where American forces under Gen. Horatio Gates met the British forces under Gen. John Burgoyne on September 9 and October 7, 1777. Gentleman Johnny's surrender to Gates on October 16 marked the first major U.S. victory of the Revolutionary War and was instrumental in bringing France into the conflict on the side of the Americans.

(*Left*) At one time several clocks such as the one pictured here dotted Broadway, Saratoga Springs' main street. Today the lone survivor stands in front of the Adirondack Trust.

(*Above*) Facing the ocean on celebrated Beach Drive is a string of resort hotels and private homes in the Victorian style for which Cape May is famous. The large structure with the red roof and awnings is the Sea Mist, an apartment building.

(*Opposite*) St. Peter's by the Sea is a summer chapel located at Cape May Point. It was built in the Stick style in 1876 and still features its original pews.

The headline read "Seashore Entertainment at Cape May," and the copy beneath it informed pleasure-seekers that "the subscriber has prepared himself for entertaining company who use sea bathing and he is accomodated with extensive house room, with fish, oysters, crabs, and good liquors— care will be taken of gentlemen's horses."

It was with this advertisement, which appeared in the *Philadelphia Aurora* in July 1801, that America's first resort town was born. By then Cape May Island, New Jersey had been inhabited by white settlers for more than a century. Discovered in 1609 by Henry Hudson, it was claimed 12 years later by Capt. Cornelius Jacobson Mey of the Dutch West India Company, who named it for himself. By 1638 it had begun to attract whalers from New England who hoped to build a new Nantucket there. They didn't. Instead, during the 18th century, the island became farmland.

Surrounded by water—the Atlantic Ocean, Cold Spring Inlet, Cape Island Creek, and another inlet which has since been filled in—the island treated visitors to pleasant surroundings and mild summer weather. Soon the word spread and men of leisure began boating over to hunt, fish,

house room" consisted of what amounted to a barn, 50-foot square and unplastered, which offered guests a common table for meals and a general sleeping area. Blankets were hung to form a barrier between the sexes.

It was left to Ellis' son, Thomas, to elevate the standard of living with a three-story structure built shortly after the War of 1812. Ellis called his hostelry the Large House, and indeed it was believed to be the biggest structure of its kind in the nation at the time, with accommodations for about a hundred people. The neighbors called it Tommy's Folly, but the Large House, renamed Congress Hall in 1828, was a success from the very start.

By the early 1820s, two more hotels had been constructed and more were on the way. Getting to the island wasn't easy. One had to come by sail, horseback, or stagecoach and the journey could take several days. But people came. By the middle of the 1830s, the island was playing host to about 700 visitors at any given time during the summer months. Many of them stayed

and relax. Typically they stayed with local farm families, who welcomed the extra income they proffered.

The "subscriber" of the *Philadelphia Aurora* notice, Ellis Hughes, merely took the next logical step—advertising. But the accommodations he provided were hardly luxurious. His "extensive

(Above) Built in 1869, the Abbey is one of Cape May's best-known inns. It actually consists of two structures. One, featuring a high tower, was built by John B. McCreary, and the other, in the Second Empire style, by McCreary's son, George.

(Right) Pictured here is the lighthouse on Cape May Point. It is no longer in use.

(*Above*) The Chalfonte Hotel, in the American Bracketed style, was built in 1876 by a local Civil War hero, Col. Henry Sawyer. It escaped the great fire of 1878 that destroyed 40 city blocks. A new wing was constructed in 1879 and 40 more rooms added nine years later.

(*Right*) The last great event of Cape May's Victorian age took place on the beach in August 1905, when the world's top race car drivers met in a $1,000 competition. The winner was Louis Chevrolet's Fiat, which set a new speed record, completing a mile in $51\frac{4}{5}$ seconds.

(*Below right*) One of the charms of Cape May is a mailbox in the form of a wicker basket with a heart-shaped cut-out. This engaging piece of American craftsmanship is outside the Mainstay Inn.

51

(Above) The Mainstay Inn began in 1872 as a clubhouse for wealthy gamblers. Built in the Italianate Villa style, it boasted 14-foot ceilings, ornate plaster mouldings, and elaborate chandeliers. It is now a bed-and-breakfast inn, whose parlor is seen here.

(Right) Many of the Mainstay's original furnishings are on view, and 8 of the 12 guest rooms feature private baths, one of which is pictured here.

This group of vacationers posed for the photographer in 1868, when Cape May was just about at the height of its popularity.

at the Mansion House, which could accommodate about 300 guests. Built in 1832, this was the first hostelry on the island to be lathed and plastered.

Thanks in large part to the advent of steamship and railway travel, Cape May reached its peak as a resort community in the 1850s, when it was drawing as many as 3,000 visitors a day in July and August. Although it faced some competition by then from Long Branch, New Jersey and Saratoga Springs, New York, its location made it particularly attractive, not only to the elite of northern cities like Philadelphia and Wilmington but also to southerners in Baltimore, Washington, D.C., and Richmond.

In 1853 the island welcomed its newest hostelry, the Mount Vernon. Named for George Washington's Virginia estate, this was Cape May's fanciest hotel yet, with elaborate ornamentation, long porches, hot and cold water, and gas lamps. The world's largest hotel at the time, it could lodge 3,500 guests and seat 2,500 at dinner.

In its heyday, Cape May played host to many of the nation's power brokers. Abraham Lincoln and his wife visited there in the 1840s, when the future president was a fledgling congressman. Henry Clay came for a week in 1847. At the time, the Great Compromiser was trying to recover from the death of his son but he was besieged by well-wishers, who failed to leave him alone even when he was bathing in the ocean. The first sitting U.S. president to visit the resort was Franklin Pierce, in 1855. Forty-five years later, President Benjamin Harrison made Congress Hall the summer White House. Other notables who vacationed on the island over the years included actress Lily Langtry, showman P. T. Barnum, novelist Owen Wister, and the founder of the American Red Cross, Clara Barton.

As Cape May's popularity grew, the range of activities and entertainments that it offered increased dramatically. One could still hunt or fish, those being the sports that had initially drawn people to the island. And, of

course, there was the ocean. On the beach the proprieties of the Victorian Age were observed. When a red flag was flying, only men could partake of the waters. When a white banner was aloft, it was the ladies' turn. In the afternoons, the men could gamble at the elaborate establishments that arose for their pleasure or practice their marksmanship skills at one of the pistol galleries. There were also bowling alleys, archery ranges, and billiard parlors. Horses could be rented for those who liked to ride on the beach and, for those who preferred to watch, trotting races were introduced at a mile-long track in 1867. Baseball became popu-

lar. In fact in 1866, two years after the sport was introduced on the island, the summer residents fielded a team against the visiting Philadelphia Athletics and lost to the pros by only four runs. In the evenings, there were balls and concerts with bands and orchestras imported from Philadelphia. Perhaps the highlight of this glittering evening fare came in August 1882 when John Philip Sousa and the Marine Band were in town. Each evening they began their concert with the March King's new composition, named for Congress Hall.

During Cape May's boom years, the community of permanent residents

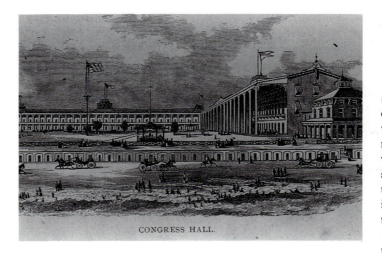

CONGRESS HALL.

(Left) **Congress Hall was expanded many times over the years, becoming one of the most celebrated hotels in the world. It even served as the summer White House during the Benjamin Harrison administration. The hotel that exists today *(below)* was built in 1879, after the previous structure burned.**

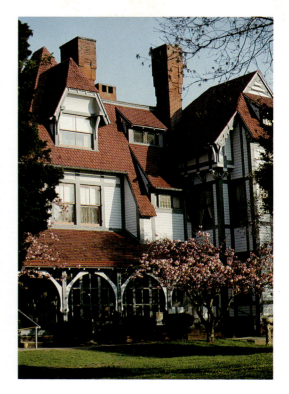

(*Above*) The home of Dr. Emlen Physick is attributed to noted architect Frank Furness. Constructed in 1878/79 in the Stick style, it is noted for its tapering chimneys, steeply gabled roofs, and irregular silhouette, all of which typify Furness' work. Today the Physick estate serves as a museum and the home of the Mid-Atlantic Center for the Arts.

Pictured here is the home of Dr. Henry Hunt, built in 1881 in the Queen Anne style. Today this home is a private residence.

remained relatively small. In the 1850s the town had only seven stores. It did, however, have four churches and a public school.

In 1869, it officially changed its name from Cape May Island to Cape May City.

By then some of the affluent summer visitors had tired of the lavish hotels and "the vulgarity of the society," to quote a prominent visitor from Philadelphia. They chose instead to build cottages of their own. In the manner of their Newport counterparts later in the century, they tried to outdo each other in the style and decor of their homes, competing among themselves for the services of the island's best carpenters and drawing upon the finest architects in Philadelphia. The most popular style to emerge among the summer residents was American Bracketed, which combined motifs from the Renaissance Revival and the Italian Villa styles. Naturally it featured elements suited to warm-weather occupancy—porches and balconies and shaded high windows.

Cape May's popularity as a resort began to decline in the decades after the Civil War. First, its southern clientele, who of course stopped coming during the war years, failed to return when the hostilities ceased. Then, in

1878, it was ravaged by fire. This was not the first time the town had been beset by flames. During one episode in 1856, the glorious Mount Vernon Hotel had burned to the ground. But the 1878 fire was by far the worst. It destroyed not only the famed Congress Hall but 30 acres of buildings. The hotel district was never the same thereafter. Finally, poor roads and competition from newer resort communities, notably Atlantic City, hurt business badly. The locals might have prevented the decline, but the internal conflict between those who lived there year-round—the only ones who could vote—and the affluent summer visitors created insurmountable barriers. Even though the latter formed a cottagers' association when the former refused to purchase adequate fire equipment, the

summer contingent lacked sufficient political power. When they failed to obtain exclusion from a new state law banning gambling and a local referendum prohibiting the sale of liquor, the resort was doomed.

Ironically it was a storm in March 1962 that helped restore Cape May to glory. After three days of hurricane-force winds and rains, which sent water gushing through the streets and resulted in the worst damage in more than a century, many of the historic structures along Beach Avenue—the once-luxurious hotels and charming Victorian cottages—were wrecked. Many citizens wanted to simply tear down what was left and start anew. But architectural historian Carolyn Pitts and a group of civic-minded citizens decided the time had come to preserve

and restore what remained of the town's rich Victorian heritage, consisting at that point of some 600 wooden structures. They were so successful that 14 years later, in October 1977, the entire city was named a National Historic Landmark. Now the once-glorious resort is glorious again. It still offers the amenities that one would expect from a summer vacation spot but it does so in a unique setting, consisting of what is arguably the largest collection of Victoriana in America.

Columbia Avenue boasts one of the finest groups of Victorian Age buildings in the United States, most of which were built in the 1890s by architect Stephen Button. Today most of these handsome structures are private homes, although a few are bed and breakfasts.

(Above) Seen in the foreground here are the pavilion and six Greek Revival buildings that comprise the Fairmount Water Works, a technological wonder of the early 19th century designed by Frederick Graff. On the rise above is the Philadelphia Museum of Art, whose Neoclassical home was begun in 1919 and completed nine years later.

(Opposite) Housed in its own pavilion since the Bicentennial in 1976, the Liberty Bell originally hung from the tower of the State House, now Independence Hall. It tolled on July 8, 1776—not July 4—to summon Philadelphians to the first public reading of the Declaration of Independence. It began to crack in the 1830s but continued in use until 1846.

It was unusually hot and humid in Philadelphia during June 1776. Still the delegates to the Second Continental Congress kept the windows of the Pennsylvania State House closed much of the time, because the warm, moist air stirred up the flies from the nearby stable. When not discussing the local discomforts, the delegates concerned themselves with Gen. George Washington's depressing reports from the field. Some, like John Adams of Massachusetts, felt that the Americans needed a reason to fight and urged the Congress to declare the 13 colonies independent of Great Britain. Others, such as John Dickinson of Pennsylvania, wondered why the colonists would want to separate themselves from the greatest nation on the face of the earth.

Before the question of American independence was put to a vote—a vote that had to be unanimous, the delegates decided—Thomas Jefferson of Virginia was asked to draft a statement that would give voice to the colonists' reasons for wanting to sever their bonds with England. The document that Jefferson drafted was masterful in its eloquence: "We hold these truths to be self-evident, that all men are created equal, that they are endowed by their Creator with

Pictured here is a view of the southeast prospect of the city around 1730 by Peter Cooper Painter. By then, Philadelphia was on its way to becoming the second largest (after Boston) seaport on the Atlantic.

The Assembly Room in Independence Hall is perhaps the most historic chamber in America, for it was here that the Declaration of Independence was signed in 1776 and the Constitution drafted in 1787.

certain unalienable rights, that among these are life, liberty, and the pursuit of happiness." After considerable debate and numerous changes to Jefferson's document, the delegates voted in favor of independence on July 4, and for the first time in history a group of colonies declared themselves free from the nation that had founded them.

The city that became known as the Birthplace of American Independence had been established 95 years earlier by a visionary who was the equal of any who attended the Second Continental Congress. The son of a celebrated admiral, William Penn was born in London in 1644 and became a militant Quaker at the age of 21. Nine years thereafter, he secured in place of a debt

owed him by the Crown a large tract of land in America. There he planned to build a community where people could live in peace and harmony. He even intended to call his capital city Philadelphia, from the Greek for "city of brotherly love."

In September 1681, Penn dispatched three representatives to ready the colony for settlement. When they arrived, however, they found no available acreage along the Delaware River, which jeopardized Penn's idea of establishing Philadelphia as a port. Finally, in early 1682, they secured from local sources a tract of riverfront property, and that summer the team's surveyor-general, Capt. Thomas Holme, laid out the city.

When Penn himself arrived several months later, he decided to expand west to the Schuylkill River, turning the city into a rectangle of 1,200 acres. His modified town plan called for uniform streets, generous-sized lots, four parks, and a 10-acre square in the center surrounded by the town's principal buildings, including the Quaker meeting house. He made no provisions for city walls or fortifications, as he intended to live in peace with the Indians and, indeed, made a treaty of friendship with the Lenni Lenape tribe in 1683.

Despite the natural obstacles confronting Philadelphia, not the least of which was the city's location a hundred miles up river from the Atlantic Ocean, the town developed into a

(Far left) Initially Independence Hall served as the Pennsylvania State House. Designed by Andrew Hamilton, an attorney and speaker of the assembly who was also an amateur architect, the brick structure with marble trim opened in 1741. The square tower was completed 12 years later.

(Top left) In 1674, Quaker William Penn acquired a large tract of American land from the British crown and determined to build on it a community where people could live in peace and harmony. He first visited the colony in 1682, laying out a modified plan for its capital, Philadelphia, shortly thereafter.

(Left) Colonial Philadelphia's most celebrated citizen was Benjamin Franklin, who arrived from Boston in 1723 at the age of 17. Among his many accomplishments were the organization of the first public library in America and the publication of the witty *Poor Richard's Almanac*. He also served as delegate to both the Second Continental Congress and the Consitutional Convention.

(Left) On the first floor of Independence Hall, opposite the Assembly Room, is the Pennsylvania Supreme Court Chamber. Philadelphia was the capital of the colony from its founding in 1681 to 1799, when Harrisburg succeeded it as the state's seat of government.

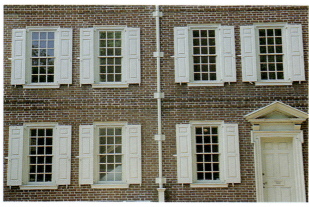

The brick townhouse pictured here was home in 1797/98 to Thaddeus Kosciusko, a Polish statesman who served as the chief engineer of the Continental Army during the Revolutionary War.

(Left) The only freestanding Federal period townhouse in Society Hill, this four-story brick structure originally belonged to Henry Hill, a wine merchant and legislator. Later occupants included Dr. Philip Syng Physick, known as the "Father of American Surgery."

(Below) In 1774 the first Continental Congress met in this cruciform-shaped building known as Carpenters' Hall, now part of Independence National Historical Park. Still owned and operated by the Carpenters' Company, which was founded in 1724, the hall served as a hospital during the Revolutionary War and later as the original quarters for the First National Bank.

major port, and soon the riverfront was dotted with wharves, warehouses, and shops.

The city was also surrounded by rich agricultural land and, as this acreage began to yield an abundance of crops under the ministrations of the new settlers, the Philadelphia merchants found a lucrative source of exports. Consequently, the town grew rapidly. From a few hundred residents in 1683, it numbered more than 2,000 by the end of the century. By 1690, there were some 22 shops and more than a hundred

Pictured here is Elfreth's Alley, a narrow passageway between Second and Front streets that includes 33 houses, some of which date to the 1720s. The oldest continuously inhabited street in Philadelphia, Elfreth's Alley was initially developed around 1702, although the man for whom it is named, Jeremiah Elfreth, didn't acquire the property until the mid-18th century.

craftsmen engaged in 35 different types of endeavor.

The Quakers predominated at first, but the colony's religious tolerance attracted people from other faiths. By 1700, members of the Society of Friends represented only about 40 percent of the population, and their presence was reduced to about 17 percent by the mid-18th century.

In 1699 Penn returned to the colony after a 15-year absence, departing for the final time two years later. Thereafter, his Pennsylvania affairs were supervised by James Logan, a former schoolteacher from Bristol. Logan was a major force in the colony for nearly 50 years, helping Philadelphia expand its economic base by, among other things, fostering the fur trade with the Indians.

Although Logan's role in colonial Philadelphia was significant, no citizen contributed more to the town's development or its reputation than Benjamin Franklin. Arriving from Boston in 1723 at the age of 17, Franklin organized a noteworthy philosophical club known as the Junto in 1727 and commenced publication two years later of the *Pennsylvania Gazette*, which many came to regard as the finest weekly newspaper in the colonies. During the ensuing decade Franklin also organized the first public library in America, published the witty *Poor Richard's Almanac*, and helped found the city's first volunteer fire brigade.

Although the city needed fire fighters, its many brick buildings preserved it from the kinds of conflagration experienced by other communities. But

(Right) In 1777, Betsy Ross was a widow living on Arch Street in Philadelphia. Her uncle by marriage was a friend of George Washington, who asked her to design a flag for the Continental army. It was at her suggestion that the stars had five instead of six points and that they were arranged in a circle.

(Above) Built in 1763/64 by a wealthy Scottish privateer, Mount Pleasant is an elegant Georgian style mansion which John Adams once called "the most elegant seat in Pennsylvania."

(Right) The interiors at Mount Pleasant mostly feature Chippendale style furniture, as seen here in the dining room located in the rear south of the residence.

Philadelphia suffered from other ills. It was dirty. And it was perhaps the most violent city in America, with numerous assaults, robberies, and burglaries. As with any other port, it had its fair share of taverns—120 by 1752. But it also had a hospital, theaters, a college, and even a dancing school, which opened in 1729.

In addition to the flourishing sea trade, which made Philadelphia the second largest (after Boston) seaport on the Atlantic by 1740, the community benefited from the westward migration that began at mid-century. Indeed, the Philadelphia Wagon Road, which emerged as the jumping off place for the pioneers, became the most heavily trafficked highway in America.

Its position as Pennsylvania's capital also helped fill the local coffers, for the shops and lodging places did a lively trade when the courts and the legislature were in session.

By 1765, the town had grown to more than 25,000 residents, making it the fourth largest city in the British empire, surpassed only by London, Edinburgh, and Dublin. Thus it was logical that Philadelphia serve as the meeting place for the first Continental Congress, held in the still incomplete Carpenters' Hall in 1774. With only Georgia unrepresented, the 56 delegates passed a resolution condemning Britain's interference in the colonies' internal affairs. With this gathering, the colonials began to think of them-

selves as Americans instead of citizens of individual colonies.

Conditions had worsened dramatically when the Second Continental Congress convened at the Pennsylvania State House (now Independence Hall) on May 8, 1775. By then, the colonies were in effect at war with Britain. The delegates' first act of business was to raise an army; several weeks later they appointed as commander a delegate from Virginia, George Washington.

Meanwhile, Philadelphia remained vulnerable to a British attack. And, indeed, on September 26, 1777, the city fell to the forces of Lord Cornwallis. Congress relocated to York, Pennsylvania and many of the town's citizens fled before the invaders, but in general Philadelphia's occupation was uneventful. Finally, on June 18, 1778, the British withdrew to reinforce New York.

In the years following the Revolutionary War, which ended in 1783, the United States' economy fell into dire straits, due largely to the weak central government created by the Articles of Confederation in 1781. A convention to revise the Articles was convened in Philadelphia in May 1787. Instead of fulfilling their mission, the delegates decided to write an entirely new Constitution. Working through another hot Philadelphia summer in the same assembly hall that had housed the Second Continental Congress, men like Alexander Hamilton of New York, James Madison of Virginia, convention president George Washington, and Dr. Franklin, then 81 years old, hammered out an entirely new system of government. The document sought to appease those who feared a strong central authority and, at the same time, alleviate the problems caused by the loose confederation. The work of the convention ended on September 17, 1787, and the Constitution, which required the ratification of nine states, took effect on July 2, 1788.

Two years later, Philadelphians rejoiced to see their city become the seat of government once more, New

(*Above*) Thomas Jefferson was only 33 years old when he drafted the Declaration of Independence, a masterful document that eloquently set forth the reasons why the 13 colonies sought to free themselves from the tyranny of King George III.

York having served as the national capital since 1785. But their hopes were dashed when Congress decided to build a new federal city along the Potomac River. In 1800 Washington, D. C. became the nation's capital and Philadelphia's days as America's premiere city were at an end. By then, Harrisburg had also superseded Philadelphia as Pennsylvania's capital.

Appropriately, the eyes of the nation again turned to the City of Brotherly Love in 1876, the 100th anniversary of America's independence. The great Centennial Exposition, the first international fair in the United States, covered more than 450 acres in Fairmount Park and cost more than $11 million. Thirty-seven nations participated in the event, but it was the display of American technology in Machinery Hall that drew the largest crowds.

Today Philadelphia is the fifth largest city in the nation with a population of more than 1.5 million. It is every inch a metropolis, but preserved in the heart of the downtown area, in Independence National Historical Park, are 26 buildings and sites that recall the early days of the republic, including Independence Hall, Carpenters' Hall, and the First Bank of the United States. Nearby are the home of Betsy Ross, reportedly the designer of the first American flag, and a modern re-creation of the place where Benjamin Franklin lived from 1763 to 1765.

Society Hill originally belonged to the Free Society of Traders, which acquired it from William Penn in 1681 as part of a tract of 20,000 acres. The Society's grand commercial schemes came to little and it ceased operations in 1686, but Society Hill blossomed as a residential district in the 1750s. A highly successful redevelopment program begun in the 1950s has restored some 800 structures in the area. Delancy Street is pictured here.

(Above) In 1769 merchant Charles Wallace purchased a tract of land between State Circle and the town dock and laid out two streets, one of which, Cornhill Street, is pictured here. Those who chose to live on this thoroughfare were mostly tradesmen and craftsmen, such as carpenter William Moore and tailor Thomas Callahan.

(Opposite) This beautiful Chinese vase in a window of the Chase-Lloyd House serves as a reminder of the days when wealthy Tidewater tobacco growers could afford to buy the high-quality, high-priced goods imported by Annapolis' leading merchants.

In 1952 a small but dedicated band of Annapolis citizens, including one very determined lady named St. Clair Wright, decided the time had come to reclaim their town from the decay into which it had fallen. The Annapolis they once knew had become something of a typical sailors' port, with a plethora of bars and taverns, adult bookstores, and glaring neon signs dominating the downtown area. But those who formed Historic Annapolis, Inc. (now the Historic Annapolis Foundation) saw past the surface squalor to the lively colonial city that had been called the Athens of America. Looking at their handiwork today, it is hard to imagine that this charming, graceful town—so redolent of a bygone age—could ever have been otherwise.

Initially Annapolis was called Arundleton by those who settled at the mouth of the Severn River, a short distance from its confluence with Chesapeake Bay. They came from Virginia in 1649, seeking religious freedom at a time when Maryland, comprising some seven million acres, had been granted by royal charter to Cecil Calvert, Lord Baltimore. A Catholic, Lord Baltimore proclaimed the colony open to

One of the major success stories of the Historic Annapolis Foundation was the William Paca House, which over the years had become a hotel completely unrecognizable as containing an 18th-century Georgian home. The demise of the hotel gave rise to a careful reconstruction of the house as well as Paca's garden, which is owned by the State of Maryland. Charles Willson Peale's portrait of the signer of the Declaration of Independence, which features Paca's garden in the background, is at right.

all who recognized the Trinity and, by way of thanks, the people of Arundleton named their town for his wife, Anne Arundel.

The growth of the new community was something less than swift. By 1694, the town still had fewer than 250 residents. In that year, Lord Baltimore lost his charter and a royal governor, Francis Nicholson, was dispatched to administer Maryland's affairs. Nicholson moved the capital of the colony from St. Mary's to Arundleton and renamed the city Annapolis, after Princess Anne, the heir to the British throne (she became queen seven years later). The governor then proceeded to lay out the town himself, anchoring his plan around two circles, one containing the State House, the other the principal church, St. Anne's. The main streets radiated from these central points, with lesser thoroughfares intersecting them at right angles.

Even after the town became the colonial capital, growth was slow, for most of the early settlers situated themselves along the riverbanks where seacraft could anchor at their private wharves. Thus the need for a trade and commercial center was minimal. The situation began to change, however, during the early years of the 18th century when the coastal lands had all been claimed and new plantations began to emerge in the interior lands.

The area's principal crop was tobacco. While the leafy plants can be grown in many places, they are fragile and may sustain appreciable damage if carted even a relatively short distance over rough roads. The Tidewater area of Maryland and Virginia, with its thousands of square miles linked by a complex system of natural waterways, was ideally suited to the transport of this cash crop. Consequently tobacco production in the area became so prolific that Maryland was annually shipping millions of pounds back to England by the 1660s.

Given the town's location and the abundance of timber, it is not surprising that shipbuilding soon became

another principal source of income. Indeed, by the middle of the 18th century, Annapolis was the foremost seaport in the colony, replete with ropewalks, ship chandleries, sailmakers' shops, ironmongeries, and other maritime businesses. Tanneries and ironworks also abounded, with Maryland exporting roughly half of all the iron produced in the colonies by the 1750s. And, of course, the business of government provided a major source of income.

As the town prospered, homes began to take on a substantial character. One of the first was an imposing brick structure built about 1727 by wealthy landowner Charles Carroll. In 1742, a new mansion for the governor was undertaken by shipbuilder Patrick

Creagh based on a plan sent from Glasgow. Funds ran out before the structure could be completed, however, and it remained unfinished for 40 years. In the custom of the day, young, prosperous attorney William Paca—later a signer of the Declaration of Independence and three-time governor of Maryland—designed his own home, basing his ideas on layouts in books. One house that was professionally designed was owned by Mathias Hammond, a wealthy planter and lawyer. This graceful Georgian structure was

Originally called Carroll's Alley, because the property here was owned by Charles Carroll, who rented it to various middle-class families, Pinkney Street is home to various clapboard row houses, most of which were built in the 1870s and 1880s.

School Street, pictured here, was one of the original thoroughfares laid out in Gov. Francis Nicholson's 1695 plan of the town. Only one structure today dates from the 18th century. The remainder were built in the 19th century, starting around 1820.

the masterpiece of British born and trained William Buckland, who came to America in 1755.

By 1774, when Buckland received the Hammond commission, Annapolis was enjoying a period of tremendous growth and development. Looking back on this Golden Age, which began about 1760, one former resident called Annapolis "the gentleelist [*sic*] town in North America."

During this era the city gained a well-deserved reputation for its lively social life. Especially during the Publik Times—those periods when the courts and the general assembly were in session—Annapolis was a bustling place indeed, filled not only with legislators, lawyers, and litigants going about their business, but also plantation owners settling into townhouses with their families to enjoy the attendant whirl of social events. There were balls, banquets, and card parties. And horse racing was so popular that Annapolis became the virtual capital of the sport for the 13 colonies.

There were clubs, like the Forensic Club, which included among its members several future signers of the Declaration of Independence, and the more frivolous Ugly Club. In the arts, the city could point to the accomplishments of portraitist Charles Willson Peale, who had been sent to London by a group of Maryland gentlemen to study under Benjamin West and who returned in 1769 to paint portraits of many of the town's leading citizens before moving to Philadelphia in 1776. The city also boasted a rich theatrical season, with several permanent theaters playing host to such notable traveling troops as the Murray-Kean Company. Shopkeepers specializing in luxury goods—such as silversmiths, watchmakers, and furniture-makers—did a lively trade. Surprisingly, they spent less time producing high-quality goods than importing such items from London, for unlike many colonists elsewhere, the leading citizens of Annapolis could afford the high price of imports in the latest fashion. Of course, after 1765, when the Stamp Act com-

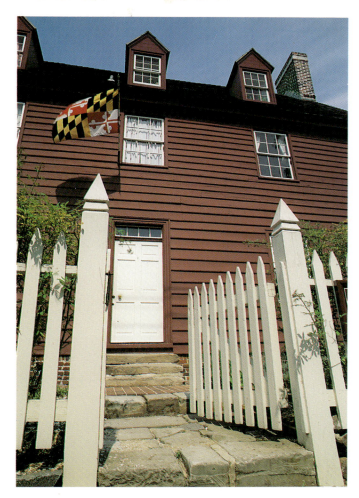

(Left) The first structure to be restored by Historic Annapolis was the Shiplap House at 18 Pinkney Street. Built about 1713, it was home between 1738 and 1748 to Ashbury Sutton, one of the city's most successful ship-builders.

(Below) Pictured here is the Old Senate Chamber as it looked in 1783/84 when the Maryland State House became the seat of the U. S. Congress. The figure of George Washington near the window recalls the moment on January 14, 1784, when the Revolutionary War hero resigned his commission here as commander-in-chief of the army.

pelled colonists to pay a special tax on all legal and commercial documents, it became the practice to boycott British merchandise in favor of items crafted locally.

The Stamp Act and other repressive measures also led to the formation of a local chapter of the Sons of Liberty.

Many of its members were not radicals. They merely believed that their rights as British subjects were being violated. The citizens of Annapolis were less sanguine by 1774, however, when they joined their counterparts in Boston and other cities in staging a "party" to protest the continuing British tax on

(Right) Begun in 1772, the Maryland State House is the oldest state capitol still in use. The octagonal dome and cupola, which can be seen from much of the city, were added in 1788 by architect Joseph Clark. The chambers where the state's bicameral legislature presently meet are part of an addition built in 1905.

(Below) The Burning of the Peggy Stewart by Frank Mayer recalls the event in October 1774, when the owner of a ship bearing 2,000 pounds of British tea destroyed his own vessel rather than face the Annapolis citizens, who were infuriated by Parliament's continuing tax on his cargo.

tea. Their anger had still not abated by October 1774, when the *Peggy Stewart* arrived in town with 2,000 pounds of tea. Rather than face local reprisals, the owner destroyed his own vessel and its contents.

During the Revolutionary War, Annapolis, like other port cities, suffered during a Royal Naval blockade, but the city was never attacked or occupied. Rather it served primarily as a supply center for the Continental Army, with food, clothing, and weapons gathered here and then shipped to the troops as needed. It was also a way station for recruits awaiting transporation to the war zone.

Annapolis' role in the national scene reached its zenith in the years immediately following the war, when the fledgling U.S. legislature took up residence in the Maryland State House from November 1783 to August 1784. During those nine months, two significant events occurred—on December 23, 1783, George Washington resigned his commission as commander-in-chief of the army, and, on January 14, 1784, Congress ratified the Treaty of Paris, formally ending the Revolutionary War. In 1786, Annapolis was also the site of a convention, which sat at Mann's Tavern, to consider the rather sorry state of U.S. trade under the Articles of Confederation. The gathering, being poorly attended, accomplished little, but from it issued a call for another convention in Philadelphia the following year. That conclave produced the U.S. Constitution.

In the ensuing years, Annapolis sought to continue as a national venue, vying with several other cities to become the nation's capital. That was not to be. It did, however, remain the capital of Maryland, despite a nearly successful attempt by Baltimore to become the seat of state government in 1786. Annapolis may have won that important battle, but it couldn't stop Baltimore, whose harbor was deeper, from succeeding it as Maryland's leading port. Thereafter Annapolis' maritime economy was largely confined to the Chesapeake Bay area. The Golden Age may have passed, but the city found renewed vigor in 1845 as the home of the U.S. Naval Academy. It has remained in Annapolis ever since, except for the Civil War years when Maryland's many southern sympathizers mandated its temporary relocation to Newport, Rhode Island.

Today Annapolis boasts more 18th-century brick buildings than any other city in America. The historic district, which was declared a National Historic Landmark in 1965, includes some 470 restored structures, several of which are open to the public. Most of the historic sites are within walking distance of one another and of the Naval Academy, and maps marking their locations are readily available in town.

(Right) This handsome three-story structure was begun in 1769 at the behest of Samuel Chase, who later sat on the U.S. Supreme Court. A lack of funds forced him to sell the then-uncompleted house two years later to a wealthy planter, Edward Lloyd IV. Today the house is known by both owners' names.

(Above) One of the most striking structures on the stately Beaux Arts campus of the U. S. Naval Academy is the chapel, begun in 1904. It features a dome that rises 200 feet above the floor and stained glass windows by Tiffany, and in the crypt beneath the chapel is the elaborate marble sarcophagus of naval hero John Paul Jones.

(Far left) Designed by architect William Buckland, the Hammond-Harwood House, completed in 1776, is generally regarded as one of the finest colonial homes in America. As with many of Annapolis' homes, it is a five-part Georgian residence, with a main house, two wings, and two connecting passageways.

(Left) Among Maryland's leading Roman Catholics was the Carroll family. Charles Carroll of Carrollton, seen here in an 1834 portrait by Thomas Sully, was a signer of the Declaration of Independence. He is believed to have been born in the Annapolis home built by his father, also named Charles, in 1727.

The South

(Above) Developed around 1785, 27th Street was originally named for President James Monroe. As did much of Georgetown, the street changed dramatically over the years. Today it primarily features row houses from the Victorian Age, the period in which Georgetown experienced a dramatic building boom.

(Opposite) This private home at 2715 Dumbarton Street looks as if it were built early in the 19th century, but in fact it was constructed in the 1940s. It replaced the original structure on the site, which was erected in 1818 and razed in 1939. The mirror likeness of this house, next door at 2713 Dumbarton Street, was once home to New York congressman Kenneth Keating.

(Previous pages) Drayton Hall, Charleston, South Carolina.

It has not been an independent city for more than 120 years, but somehow amid all the nearby symbols of national significance—the White House, the U.S. Capitol, the Washington Monument, and the Lincoln Memorial—Georgetown has managed to retain its own, unique identity. Some know it as the place where Senator John F. Kennedy and his wife Jacqueline were living when he was elected president. Others recall it as the setting of the horrific doings in *The Exorcist*. To others still it is the home of a major university and the site of sophisticated restaurants and shops.

The land that gave rise to the town was originally in Maryland. One of the first settlers was a Scot named Ninian Beall, who arrived in the New World around 1658. By the beginning of the 18th century, he had become a man of property, including some 795 acres near the fall line of the Potomac River. A high promontory on the grounds reminded him of the Rock of Dumbarton near Glasgow, so he named the estate after the Scottish landmark.

By the early 18th century other plantation owners had settled in the area and tobacco had become the principal crop. Among the planters was Beall's neighbor, George

(Left) For 179 years Tudor Place was home to members of a single family, the Peters. The original owner was Thomas Peter, the son of a successful tobacco merchant and Georgetown's first mayor. His wife was Martha Custis, a granddaughter of Martha Washington.

(Below) Built on the crest of Georgetown Heights, the impressive Neoclassical Tudor Place was completed in 1816. Among the estate's most notable features is its expansive gardens, which reflect the original plantings and designs of the Federal period and those added by succeeding generations of Peters.

Gordon, who in the 1740s established a tobacco inspection station on his Rock Creek Plantation. Then, in 1747, a tavern opened nearby. Commercial activity within the area increased significantly thereafter and in 1751, the local plantation owners petitioned the Maryland Assembly for a charter establishing a town. Surveyors appointed by the legislature determined that portions of the Beall estate, then owned by Ninian's son, George, and Gordon's adjacent property represented the best location for the settlement. In exchange for their holdings, each man was offered £240 and his choice of two town lots.

The new community was named George Town*, for the reigning monarch, George II. It initially comprised 60 acres, divided into 80 lots along a gridded plan. Such was its success that all but 11 lots sold at the first offering, which took place in March 1752.

Given its location on the Potomac River, which feeds into Chesapeake Bay, Georgetown quickly emerged as a major port, becoming by the end of the 18th century the premiere tobacco market in Maryland. In those days it was a lively place indeed, with a host of shops and taverns. In time its ships traveled not only to England but also to other colonial ports, including Salem, Massachusetts. They even journeyed to the West Indies. In exchange for tobacco and locally grown wheat, they brought back sugar, molasses, and rum and, from England, fine furnishings and apparel. The local merchants happily displayed their wealth in homes that were suited to their stations. Indeed, they so impressed Gen. Edward Braddock, the British commander of the troops in Virginia, that he

* The one- and two-word spellings of the town name were used somewhat interchangeably until about the mid-19th century when the one-word spelling began to predominate. For consistency the one-word spelling will be used hereafter in the text.

(Left) Gilbert Stuart, the foremost painter of the Federal period, was a resident of Georgetown for around two years starting in 1803. He is best known today for his portraits of George Washington and the presidents who followed him.

(Above) Colorful flower boxes, a wrought-iron railing, and red brick with white window guards leave to the imagination the rest of this stately house on N Street.

(Left) Begun in 1828, the Chesapeake and Ohio Canal was originally intended to extend from Georgetown to Pittsburgh and the Ohio Valley, but it never went further west than Cumberland, Maryland. Today the canal, which is operated by the National Park Service, is a favorite spot for joggers and canoeists and provides a scenic backdrop for a number of restaurants.

One of the first settlers in the area that became Georgetown was a Scot named Ninian Beall, who arrived in the New World around 1658. When the town was established in 1751, part of his estate—then held by his son, George—was chosen for the townsite.

In the landmark case, Marbury v. Madison, Georgetown resident William Marbury sued the secretary of state, James Madison, over a political appointment, and Chief Justice John Marshall, pictured here, established the Supreme Court as the final arbiter of the Constitution.

wrote in 1775, ". . . never have I attended a more complete banquet, or met better dressed or better mannered people than I met on my arrival in George Town."

During the Revolutionary War, Georgetown served as a major port from which supplies—livestock, wag-ons, gunpowder, and medicines—were shipped to the forces at the front. In 1789, six years after the conclusion of the conflict, the town was incorporated. That year also saw the establishment of the first local newspaper, the *Times and Potomac Packet*, which was joined by the *Weekly Ledger* in 1790. Within a few years, the community also boasted a mill, a gun factory, and its first bank, the Bank of Columbia.

By then, however, Georgetown's days as a totally independent community were numbered. It was in 1790 that the U. S. Congress, meeting in Philadelphia, decided that the new nation should have its own capital city and that it should be located along the Potomac. It was left to President George Washington, who was a trained surveyor, to select the exact site. On March 30, 1791, after meeting with the local landholders and city commissioners in Georgetown, the chief executive announced the boundaries of the 10-square-mile capital. Georgetown and Alexandria, Virginia were to be part of the federal district but would retain their status as independent municipalities.

Initially the citizens of Georgetown were happy about the situation, believing that their association with the District of Columbia would yield additional income without infringing upon their freedom. Many of them even journeyed to the developing federal city on September 18, 1793, to participate in the ceremony at which President Washington laid the ceremonial cornerstone for the new capitol. When the legislators arrived in 1800, many of them chose to live in the sophisticated village of nearly 3,000 even though it was a three-mile coach ride to the capitol. It had elegant shops, theaters, artisans, artists, even a college, which opened in 1789 (it became Georgetown University in 1815). Comparing the established port city to the newly built capital, one early visitor wrote, "It is hardly possible to conceive how towns so near each other should differ so widely as they do."

Among those who settled here in 1803 was Gilbert Stuart, the foremost painter of the Federal period. That same year another local resident, William Marbury, sued the secretary of state, James Madison, over the latter's failure to honor the judicial appointment bestowed on him by outgoing

president John Adams. In hearing *Marbury v. Madison* Chief Justice John Marshall established two fundamental principals of the American political system, that the Supreme Court is the final interpreter of the Constitution and that it has the right to rule on the constitutionality of legislation.

Another early-19th-century Georgetown resident was Philadelphia armorer Henry Foxall, who came to the District of Columbia in 1799 to build an ordinance plant for the nation's capital.

In 1814, during the War of 1812, the British sacked Washington, burning, among other things, the White House

With its colorful Federal style row houses, N Street is one of Georgetown's most charming residential thoroughfares. It was originally known as Gay Street west of what is now Wisconsin Avenue—the old Indian trail over which plantation owners brought their tobacco into town—and First Street to the east. Senator Robert F. Kennedy made his home here at the time of his assassination.

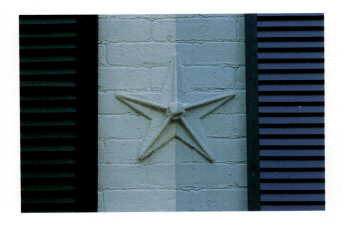

(*Top*) Decorative stars like the one pictured here are commonplace in Georgetown. They were used in the restoration of buildings to hold the brickwork in place.

(*Above*) An early-19th-century Georgetown resident was Philadelphia armorer Henry Foxall, who built an ordinance plant for the nation's capital in 1799. It was this foundry that drew British troops to Georgetown during the War of 1812, but they were diverted by bad weather before reaching the village.

(*Right*) Thomas Jefferson Street, pictured here, was initially developed for residences around 1795. Named for the third president of the United States, who lived in Georgetown prior to becoming chief executive, the street today is a mixture of commercial establishments and homes.

(then called the President's Mansion). Foxall's Columbia Foundry drew them to Georgetown, but before they could reach the village a violent storm arose, and they were diverted.

During the first two decades of the 19th century the port of Georgetown continued to prosper, augmented by the merchants' involvement with the western fur trade. But in the 1820s the river became clogged with silt and the larger vessels then plying the seas required a deeper harbor. The city commissioners hoped to preserve the community's role

The charming brick structure at 1301 28th Street dates from about 1816, when it was built by John Yerby. It has been enlarged since then and the entrance, pictured here, has been moved around the corner from its original location. Today the home is a private residence.

in trade, at least within the Chesapeake Bay area and the Ohio River valley, by means of the Chesapeake and Ohio Canal, which was started in 1828 with Georgetown as its eastern terminus. But the canal, which was intended to reach Pittsburgh, was never completed; it only extended as far as Cumberland, Maryland, some 180 miles away. Still it did bring a measure of prosperity to the village as well as power for the mills and factories that rose beside it.

The Civil War marked a particularly difficult period in the history of Georgetown, which had a large contingent of southern sympathizers. During the conflict, the local Holy Trinity Church became a hospital ministering to the wounded of both sides, and Forrest Hall, which had been an auditorium, served as a federal prison.

The end of the war ushered in a period of local prosperity, but in 1871, amid a building and population boom, Georgetown lost its status as an independent municipality. It was congressional passage of the Territorial Act that repealed the charters of both Georgetown and the City of Washington and established instead a single governmental structure for the entire District of Columbia. This legislation marked the culmination of a long-standing conflict between the two communities. As early as 1803, Congress had deprived Georgetown residents, as well the citizens of Alexandria, Virginia of the right to vote in national elections. They were also denied representation in Congress. Alexandria successfully returned to Virginia in 1846, but Georgetown, despite repeated attempts to rejoin Maryland, remained tied to the District of Columbia.

This stately, two-story residence is known as the Old Stone House. Built around 1765, it was home to furniture-maker Christopher Layman, who, in keeping with the custom of the colonial era, lived upstairs and maintained his place of busines on the ground floor. Today it is the oldest extant building in the District of Columbia, and is open to the public under the auspices of the National Park Service.

The Territorial Act was repealed in 1874 and the legislation that replaced it, the Organic Act, was eventually discarded as well. Still, for all practical purposes, Georgetown ceased to be an independent entity in 1871. But thanks to Rock Creek, which physically separates the community from Washington, and the town's distinctive physical appearance, the result of a preservation effort that began around 1915, Georgetown has retained its independent character. Today it serves a significant role in the life of the capital. With its stately old homes and commercial structures, it complements the hallowed institutions and monuments to great leaders by reminding visitors of the nation's past as it was lived by ordinary people. Georgetown became a National Historic District in 1958.

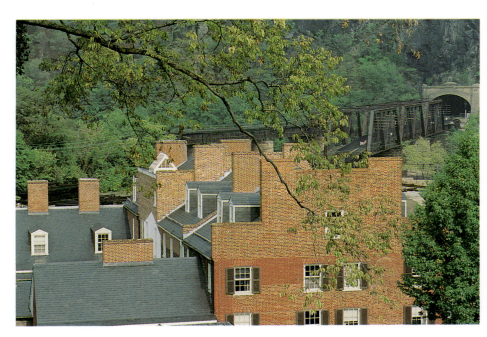

(*Above*) In the right background of this photo one can see the trestle of the Baltimore & Ohio Railroad, which reached the Maryland shore opposite Harpers Ferry in 1834. Three years later the completion of a bridge enabled the B&O to cross the Potomac. It was this structure that John Brown's men captured at the outset of their raid in 1859.

(*Opposite*) In 1859, the armory firehouse—known today as John Brown's Fort—became the last refuge of the fiery abolitionist when his plans for a slave rebellion failed. On October 18, U.S. marines under Robert E. Lee stormed the structure and captured Brown.

Age had left him bent and thin, and his once-dark, close-cropped hair had turned white. But the fire in John Brown's eyes had not dimmed, and the beard—grown to disguise his hawk-like features —made him look like an Old Testament prophet. Born in Connecticut in 1800, Brown had been a tanner, a real estate speculator, and a sheep rancher, but after 1837 the abolitionist movement became his all-consuming passion. By 1859, he had already given much to the cause, having served as the leader of a guerrilla band during the bloody battle between pro- and anti-slavery forces in Kansas. The summer of 1859 found him on a rented farm in Maryland, five miles outside of Harpers Ferry, Virginia. There he was preparing for the culmination of his divinely inspired mission—the start of a slave rebellion that would free every African-American in the South. "When I strike, the bees will swarm," he predicted.

The target of John Brown's raid was named for Robert Harper, a Philadelphia architect. In 1747, he was engaged by a group of Quakers to build a meeting house near what is presently Winchester, Virginia. His journey took him past a gap in the Blue Ridge Mountains to a place at the

(Above) Parked before the John Brown Fort is a wagon like the one that accompanied the abolitionists from their rented farm in Maryland to Harpers Ferry on October 16, 1859.

(Right) The view from St. Peter's Church, which is outside the confines of the national park, shows structures within the historic preserve. These carefully restored brick houses and commercial establishments give the impression of a tidy, prosperous Shenandoah Valley town in the 1850s.

confluence of the Shenandoah and Potomac rivers known as the "Hole." There he made the acquaintance of a squatter named Peter Stephens, who ran a rather primitive ferry service. Taken with the area's commercial and industrial promise as well as its natural beauty, Harper acquired Stephens' operation. In time, he added 125 acres of land and a gristmill to his holdings

Thirteen years after Harper's death in 1782, President George Washington selected the "Hole"—called Harpers Ferry by then—as the site for a federal armory. A factory, workshops, a work-

ers' barracks, and an arsenal for storing the completed weapons were constructed, along with a dam and canal on the Potomac River, and arms production commenced in 1801.

The success of the operation was spurred by John H. Hall, who patented the first weapon to use interchangeable parts. One thousand units of his breech-loading rifle were produced at Harpers Ferry in 1825; another thousand were assembled within the two succeeding years. By then, the armory included 20 workshops, two arsenals, 86 employee dwellings, and 271 work-

(Above) During the first half of the 19th century, Harpers Ferry emerged as a significant industrial center and transportation hub. The cornerstone of the town's economy was the federal armory, which had produced some 600,000 weapons between 1802 and the start of the Civil War. At its peak, it employed about half of the community's eligible work force.

(Left) The place at the confluence of the Shenandoah and Potomac rivers, originally known as the "Hole," was occupied by a squatter named Peter Stephens. Stephens' rather primitive ferry service was acquired in 1747 by architect Robert Harper, the man for whom the town was named.

(Right) During the Civil War, Harpers Ferry—with its key transportation network—was occupied and re-occupied by armies of both sides. In this sketch by A.E. Ward the arsenal has become a storehouse for the federal troops under Philip Sheridan.

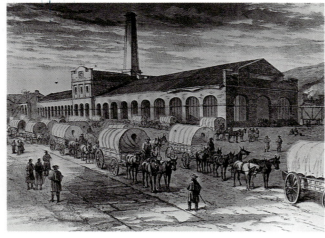

(Below) In 1859, when this photo was taken, John Brown, a Connecticut-born abolitionist, attempted to start a massive slave revolt by seizing the federal arsenal at Harper's Ferry. He failed and was hanged.

ers. So successful was the enterprise that by 1860 more than 600,000 pistols and rifles had been manufactured at Harpers Ferry and about half of the town's work force earned its living at the armory.

Meanwhile, other local industries had developed at Virginius Island a short distance from town. These included an iron foundry, a cotton mill, a flour mill, and a carriage manufacturing shop. Harpers Ferry had also emerged as a major transportation hub, a place initially traversed by overland roads and canals and later by railroads. All of this activity had brought some 1,377 people to the community by 1820. In 1859, the town, which had incorporated eight years earlier, boasted a population of about 3,000.

It was the arsenal that attracted John Brown to Harpers Ferry, but the community's location also offered a suitable place from which to carry the slave rebellion south. Moreover, the nearby mountains yielded numerous hiding places and provided access, should it become necessary, to Pennsylvania and the North.

At last Brown was ready. On Sunday night, October 16, 1859, he left the Maryland farm, bound for Harpers Ferry with 18 men, including two of his three sons (the third remained at the farm). First they seized a watchman guarding the bridge over the Potomac and then they captured the armory, overpowering its sole guard. This became Brown's headquarters, from which he dispatched his supporters with instructions to cut the town's telegraph wires and to gather hostages and slaves.

Shortly before 1:30 in the morning, a train heading toward Baltimore was stopped outside of town. Shots were

exchanged and the baggagemaster, a free black man, was mortally wounded. This melee alerted some of the townsfolk to the capture of the arsenal, and by daybreak armed citizens began to converge on Brown's stronghold. Meanwhile the militia began organizing in Charles Town, the county seat, and when it arrived the bridge over the Potomac was seized and Brown's avenue of retreat cut off. During the course of the day, October 17, shots were periodically fired between the two sides and several people—including Brown's two sons—were killed or mortally wounded.

Finally, late in the afternoon, after two unsuccessful attempts to negotiate a truce, Brown retreated with the remainder of his raiders and their hostages to the arsenal's firehouse. By then, President James Buchanan had learned of the raid—although the accounts that reached him were greatly exaggerated—and he dispatched to Harpers Ferry a force of marines under the command of Lt. Col. Robert E. Lee and Lt. J. E. B. Stuart. On October 18, the marines attacked the firehouse and quickly subdued the raiders. In all, ten of Brown's men had been killed during the raid, five—including the old patriarch—were taken prisoner, and the rest escaped.

A week later Brown went on trial in Charles Town, was convicted of treason, murder, and inciting a slave insurrection and was hanged on December 2. Many in the North praised his zeal,

As a major transportation center between the 1830s and 1861, Harpers Ferry saw a wide range of goods pass through its terminals. Local water power also gave rise to considerable industrial production whose output was also shipped via the town's canal and rails.

while those in the South were infuriated by the ill-conceived slave rebellion that he had sought to foster.

On his way to the gallows, Brown had predicted that "the crimes of this guilty land will never be purged away but with blood" and he was right. During the four years of bloody civil war, Harpers Ferry—with its key transportation network—became a focal point of the conflict. In fact, it took less than 24 hours after Virginia's secession from the Union on April 17, 1861, for Southern troops to converge on the community. Unable to defend the town, the small contingent of federals stationed there set fire to the arsenal and destroyed nearly 15,000 weapons. The citizens of Harpers Ferry, however, saved most of the armory buildings from the flames. The Southern forces held sway for almost two months, during which they stripped the armory of its useful machinery and destroyed the railroad bridge. Then, on June 15, they headed south, only to return four months later to destroy the area's remaining industrial capabilities. The Union army, which also did its share of local damage, reoccupied the town in February 1862, but September saw their force of 14,000 badly outnumbered by the Confederates under Maj. Gen. Thomas Jackson. Stonewall's ability to secure Harpers Ferry for the South helped Lee confront the Yankees at the Battle of Antietam. It also resulted in the capture of 12,500 Union officers and men, the largest such U.S. capitulation during the war.

Less than a week after Stonewall's capture of Harpers Ferry, the town was back in Union hands. This time federal troops retained control of the town until June–July 1863, when it fell briefly during the Gettysburg campaign. Again, during the summer of 1864, the Confederates regained control under Gen. Jubal Early. Federal forces reasserted themselves on July 8, however, and finally the seesaw battle came to an end. In all, Harpers Ferry had changed hands eight times during the war. By the time the conflict ended, it was no longer even a part of

(Left) Shenandoah Street, pictured here, is one of the main thoroughfares in the national historical park at Harpers Ferry. It houses the Stagecoach Inn, now the park's information center; the blacksmith shop; and the John Brown Museum.

(Above) During the Civil War Harpers Ferry became the object of a seesaw battle between the Union and the Confederacy, with both sides wreaking havoc on the town. Pictured here are the ruins of St. John's Episcopal Church.

(Left) The Frankel Brothers, who operated a store in Harpers Ferry between 1858 and 1860, sold a wide range of merchandise, including men's and boy's shirts, underwear, boots, hats, handkerchiefs, and suspenders. Jewelry and men's cologne were also available.

Virginia, whose western counties had seceded from the commonwealth to form their own state in 1863.

What had been a town of 3,000 people before the war had scarcely 300 residents left afterward. The railroad lines had been wrecked, most of the town's buildings ruined, and the armory completely destroyed. Given the total devastation, the federal government decided not to rebuild the weapons plant and little else in the way of industry returned. However, the town did give rise to an important school for African-Americans, Storer College, which remained open until 1955.

At present, there are about 400 people in the community and the town's primary industry is tourism. Much of Harpers Ferry is part of a national historical park, administered by the National Park Service. Here buildings have been restored to their 19th century appearance and townsfolk, dressed in period clothing, help to interpret a bygone age. Not only does Harpers Ferry recall the days when a young American nation embarked on significant growth in industry and transport, it also serves as a vivid reminder of a zealot named Brown who pointed the way toward a devastating war.

(Above) The Bonner House, built around 1830, is an excellent example of North Carolina coastal architecture, which features a large porch on the front of a structure and another on the rear. The rear porch is clearly visible in this photo.

(Opposite) One of the oldest extant homes in North Carolina, the Palmer-Marsh House is distinguished by this double chimney, which is 17 feet wide and four feet thick at its base.

According to legend, the bustling colonial community of Bath, North Carolina was visited in the mid-18th century by a fiery preacher named George Whitfield. Treated poorly by the local citizens, the English revivalist put a curse on the town, condemning it to be a small village forever. The story is probably untrue, for Whitfield made Bath his gospel headquarters in 1747/48 and seemed to have had no trouble conducting his ministry there, but the legend would explain how a community which had once shown such promise had become a quaint footnote in the history of the Tar Heel State.

Settlers began arriving in the northeastern part of what would become North Carolina during the 1690s. Among them were bands of French Huguenots seeking religious freedom and farmers drawn to the area's rich soil and expansive grazing land. A natural harbor on the Pamlico River attracted those with an interest in the maritime trades.

Among the earliest arrivals was an intelligent, capable Englishman by the name of John Lawson, who had come to map the province and explore the interior for the Lord Pro-

Harding's Landing on Bath Creek honors
Edmund Hart Harding, whose strong interest
in preserving the town's historic heritage gave
rise in 1959 to the Historic Bath Commission. Harding was the organization's first
chairman.

prietors, a group of English noblemen then charged with administering parts of the Carolinas (they sold their interests in 1729, after which North Carolina became a royal colony). Vigorous, charming, and possessed of wide-ranging interests, Lawson set out from Charleston in December 1700, accompanied on his mission by five other Englishmen and four Native Americans, one of whom was a woman. For four weeks they traveled the backwoods on foot and by canoe, arriving on February 23, 1701, at the Pamlico River plantation of Richard Smith. There Lawson decided to make his home. By 1704, he was surveying a town in the area. When it was incorporated as Bath in March 1705, it became the first municipality in North Carolina. At the time, it boasted at least 12 houses and probably featured stores and warehouses, primarily those associated with the sea trade. There were also boat builders, a cooper, a doctor, and a horse-driven gristmill.

The town founders were determined to make their community a pleasant place in which to live. Residents were required to keep their lands cleared of underbrush, livestock were not allowed

Among the pirates who plied the waters around Bath was Edward Teach, the tall, well-dressed and hearty brigand known as Blackbeard, seen here in a modern-day artist's rather fanciful portrait.

This rather primitive drawing shows the capture of John Lawson, surveyor general of the colony, in 1711. Although he was put to death, thereby becoming the first casualty in the four-year-long Tuscarora War, his companions, Baron Christopher de Graffenfried and a black servant, also shown here, were allowed to live. They warned other settlers of the impending conflict.

to run free, and fencing requirements were established. A common at the northern end of town at once gave residents a park, a pasture, and a place for gathering wood. Space was also reserved for such future institutions as a church, a courthouse, and a marketplace.

Soon the wharf was bustling with ships loading and unloading goods. The post route that wended from Portland, Maine to Savannah, Georgia was re-routed through Bath, giving the local economy a major boost.

In the years to come Lawson would author a book on the natural history and settlement of North Carolina, which would be published in London. And he would become the colony's surveyor general. In this capacity, he would lay out another town, New Bern. He would meet an unfortunate end, however. In 1711, while on a surveying expedition, he was captured and put to death by a band of Tuscarora Indians. Ironically, he had been warmly disposed toward the Native Americans and had even included samples of their language in his book.

(Right) This foyer in the Bonner House must have been a busy place in the 1830s, when it was home to Joseph Bonner, his wife, their six children, and their servants. The house remained in the Bonner family until the 1950s.

Lawson's death marked the start of what became known as the Tuscarora War. On September 22, 1711, some 500 Indians led by their chief, King Hancock, attacked settlers in the Pamlico region, killing nearly 200 men, women, and children and burning numerous houses and fields. Bath, which escaped the onslaught, became a place of refuge for the survivors of the three-day massacre. The whites fought back, aided by South Carolina forces under Capt. John Barnwell, who was dubbed Tuscarora Jack. The conflict between the settlers and the Indians continued periodically for four years, until a treaty was signed with the Tuscarora Nation in 1715.

The end of the Indian war brought prosperity as well as peace. But two years later, Bath faced a new problem—what to do about the many pirates preying upon ships in its waters.

A solution came in the summer of 1718, when King George I announced that he would grant amnesty to any buccaneer willing to give up piracy. Among those who came to Bath to take advantage of the king's offer was Edward Teach, better known as Blackbeard. Tall, well-dressed, and hearty and with a long, braided beard, the notorious brigand received the king's pardon and then ostensibly settled down to married life with a 16-year-old-beauty on some land south of town. In truth, however, he kept his pirate crew nearby and his ships anchored in a convenient cove, known today as Teach's Hole, and when he became restless, he resumed his wicked ways. After one stint at sea, he notified Charles Eden, the governor who had arranged his pardon, that he had found

(Above) In the kitchen of the Bonner House, one can see some of the utensils that were used for cooking in the 1830s. Until the advent of the stove in the mid-19th century, the means of preparing meals had changed very little for centuries.

(Right) Descended from the town's first county sheriff, Joseph Bonner, the original owner of the Bonner House, became a wealthy plantation owner. By the 1850s, he had more than 3,000 acres of land and 33 slaves.

(Opposite) The Van Der Veer House, the most recent structure to be restored in Bath, dates from around 1790. It is named for Jacob Van Der Veer, who acquired the house in 1824 and lived in it for 12 years.

(Right) Squash plants climbing the fence behind the Van Der Veer House add a festive note of color to the early fall setting. The house originally stood on the waterfront at the north edge of town and was moved to its present location near the Visitors Center and the Palmer-Marsh House in 1970.

Built in 1734, St. Thomas Church is the oldest existing church in North Carolina. It features walls of solid brick, two feet thick and laid in Flemish bond. The structure was named to the National Register of Historic Places in 1970.

(Below) More than 250 years after it was built, St. Thomas Episcopal Church remains an active house of worship. Much of the interior was changed in the late 19th century to reflect the tastes of the Victorian Age.

an abandoned French merchant ship and asked for salvage rights. Eden was nonplused by Teach's dubious story, perhaps because, as some have speculated, he was on Blackbeard's payroll. But the governor of Virginia, Alexander Spotswood, was not so sanguine. Facing possible impeachment for his lavish expenditures and the land grants that he had taken for himself, he saw in Blackbeard's actions a means of rallying popular support for his administration. Accordingly, he dispatched to Bath two sloops under the command of a British regular, Lt. Robert Maynard, with orders to stop the pirate. Maynard engaged Teach and his crew in hand-to-hand combat at Oracoke, the pirate's island headquarters, and when the lieutenant sailed into Bath several days later, he displayed Blackbeard's bloody head from the bowsprit of his sloop.

Perhaps it was just as well that Blackbeard didn't live to stand trial. Had he been brought to Bath, the citizens would have had difficulty deciding where to stage the event, for the town had no courthouse in 1718, even though the general assembly had provided for the construction of such an edifice three years earlier. Finally, a courthouse *was* built in 1723. Eleven years later, work began on another institution, St. Thomas Church, one of the earliest houses of worship in the colony. St. Thomas was particulary noted for its distinguished library of some 1,000 volumes, purchased in London long before the church was built. Indeed, for many years, the parish featured the only public library in North Carolina. Still in service today, St. Thomas is the oldest extant church in the Tar Heel State.

The first rector of St. Thomas was the Reverend James Garzia, who could barely speak English. After he was killed in a fall from his horse in 1744, Bath was without a minister until 1753, when a 33-year-old Irishman named Alexander Stewart became rector. The energetic Stewart not only saw to the completion of the church, whose progress had been halted upon Garzia's

(Below) The Palmer-Marsh House on Main Street was built in 1744 and acquired 20 years later by Robert Palmer, the customs collector for the port at Bath and surveyor general of the colony, whose portrait appears at left. In 1802, merchants Jonathan and Daniel Marsh became the new owners.

death, he also established the first free school in the colony.

In 1753, the year of Stewart's arrival in Bath, another distinguished citizen settled in the community. Twenty-eight-year-old Robert Palmer, who had been a lieutenant colonel in the British army, had been dispatched to North Carolina to become the customs collector for the port at Bath and surveyor general of the colony. His home was one of the first structures to be restored by the Historic Bath Commission, an organization founded in 1959 to preserve the town's historic buildings.

By the time that Stewart and Palmer became residents, Bath's glory days were behind it. Sandbars and treacherously shallow waters kept the harbor from ever becoming a grand port of entry and, when the Old Post Road was re-routed, the town lost its status as a crossroads for overland travelers. In 1746, New Bern was chosen as the colony's capital instead of Bath and in 1785, the town of Washington, founded in 1776, took over as the seat of Beaufort County. With that blow, Bath's leadership role was at an end. Still, the town has survived. Today, it is a charming village with a number of structures recalling life in the 18th century. In addition to St. Thomas Church and the Palmer-Marsh House, several restored homes are open for tours.

(Above) There are almost 2,000 restored buildings in Charleston's historic district. Many of them are private residences, like those pictured here along what is appropriately called Rainbow Row.

(Opposite) The First Presbyterian Church, also known as Scots Church, dates from 1713, but the present structure was built in 1814. During the Civil War, the congregation gave its bells to the Confederacy, which melted them down and used the raw material for munitions.

It was occupied by the British during the Revolutionary War. It was assaulted for 587 days by Union forces during the War Between the States. And it has been visited by fires, earthquakes, and some 90 hurricanes, including Hugo in 1989, which caused billions of dollars worth of property damage. In sum, Charleston, South Carolina just may have endured more during its 321-year history than any other city in America. But, like Job, it has emerged from each catastrophe with its spirit intact.

The city's origins date to April 1670, when a group of 160 settlers established an outpost at what became known as Albemarle Point. They named their settlement Charles Town, for the then-monarch of Great Britain, King Charles II. It was the first community in Carolina, which became two separate colonies—North Carolina and South Carolina—in 1710.

Ten years after its founding, the town was moved for reasons of health and safety. The new site on a peninsula between the Ashley and Cooper Rivers was laid out according to a plan sent from London. A wall surrounded the inhabitants to protect them from Indians, pirates, and

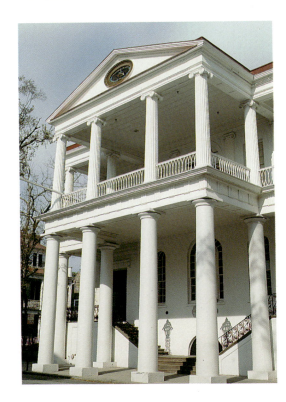

(Left) South Carolina Society Hall at 72 Meeting Street was designed by Gabriel Manigault and built in 1804. The portico by Frederick Wesner was added in 1825.

(Below) Drayton Hall, considered the earliest and finest example of Georgian-Palladian architecture in America, was built between 1738 and 1742. Union troops spared it during the Civil War because they believed it had been converted to a hospital. It was the only Ashley River plantation house to survive the Yankee torches.

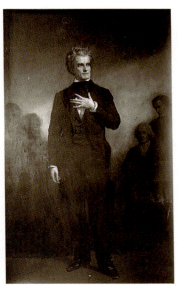

(Left) In the decades leading up to the Civil War the advocates of states rights had no greater champion than South Carolina's John C. Calhoun, who served during his career as U. S. senator, secretary of war, secretary of state, and vice-president.

the Spanish, whose New World lands were not far away.

Despite the potential dangers, the town continued to grow. By 1690, it boasted between 1,000 and 1,200 residents, making it the fifth largest settlement in the colonies. Settlers came here from a wide range of locales, including Germany, France, and the Netherlands, attracted by Carolina's distinctive practice of religious toleration.

From the beginning, Charles Town was a center for trade and shipping, and by 1720, its port was a lively place indeed, with 150 or more ships in the harbor at any one time. Pirates who tried to interfere with the shipping

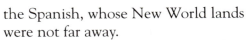

lanes soon discovered that Charles Town shipowners could not be cowed. Their retaliatory raids resulted in the execution of 49 buccaneers in one year alone.

Initially, Charles Town trafficked in furs and timber, but a series of money crops soon yielded even greater profits. The first was rice, which was ideally suited to the colony's coastal lowlands and marshes. Unlike their counterparts in nearby Virginia, the local plantation owners did not live on their estates year-round. Rather, the threat of malaria led them to establish summer homes in the city. Built for South Carolina's heat and humidity, these structures typically featured thick walls, large windows, high ceilings, and porches known as *piazzas*.

By the middle of the 18th century, Charles Town had become a sophisticated city, with race tracks, libraries, and theaters. Many of its leading citizens traveled abroad and sent their youngsters to be educated in England. And their extensive trade with the mother country—six times what it was with other local ports—kept them abreast of fashions and mores in the land that some still thought of as home. Despite Charles Town's passion for things British—which earned it the nickname "Little London"—imports from abroad were very expensive, so local equivalents often had to do. Consequently, hundreds of craftsmen settled in Charles Town during the 18th century. There were more than 250 reputable furniture-makers alone, including the noted Thomas Elfe.

Despite a devastating fire in 1740 and a severe hurricane 12 years later, the town boasted a population of 12,000 by 1773 and was the busiest port in the colonies, surpassing even Boston. In that same year, a group of Charles Town citizens founded the first museum in America and a collection of local businessmen formed the first Chamber of Commerce. The city was so grand that it prompted one New England visitor to write that it "far surpasses all I ever saw, or ever expect to see, in America."

(Left) When the Civil War ended, Charleston—the object of a 587-day Union siege—was in ruins. What had been a bustling city of some 40,000 people in 1860 was now little more than a ghost town.

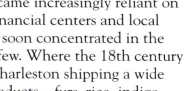

(Above) The Joseph Manigault House, circa 1803, was designed by the owner's brother, the prominent Charleston architect Gabriel Manigault. The near-destruction of this home in 1920 gave birth to Charleston's historic preservation movement.

(Left) The interiors of the Nathaniel Russell House, including the dining room pictured here, feature outstanding examples of American decorative arts from the 18th and early 19th centuries. The house was built around 1809 for Nathaniel Russell, son of a chief justice of Rhode Island.

But also by 1773, many in Charles Town had come to resent the restrictions placed upon them by the British. In December of that year, they followed Boston's example and stole a shipment of highly taxed British tea from their harbor. Instead of throwing it into the sea as the Bostonians had done, they hid it in the cellars of the Mercantile Exchange and later sold it to raise funds for the war effort.

Finally, on June 28, 1776, armed conflict erupted between the citizens of Charles Town and the forces of George III, when the British attacked a partially built fort in the harbor. A few hundred Americans with 31 cannon successfully stood against nine British men-of-war and 2,000 soldiers. Their

victory under Col. William Moultrie was America's first successful land-and-sea action during the Revolutionary War. Despite this success, however, Charles Town fell to the British on May 12, 1780. For two-and-a-half years, enemy forces remained in the town, commandeering the finest homes and imprisoning the local Patriot leaders.

The city, which changed its name to Charleston in 1783, never truly regained its pre–Revolutionary War glory. It became increasingly reliant on northern financial centers and local wealth was soon concentrated in the hands of a few. Where the 18th century had seen Charleston shipping a wide range of products—furs, rice, indigo,

(Left) Ft. Sumter in Charleston harbor was a partially completed fortress in December 1860 when it became a place of refuge for Maj. Robert Anderson and his federal troops in the wake of South Carolina's secession from the Union. It was here on April 12, 1861, that the first shots of the Civil War were fired.

(Below) Three cannon stand today along the Battery near the waterfront. This 1,500-foot walkway serves as a sea wall and a promenade. Two of the cannon originally saw action at Ft. Sumter during the Civil War.

tobacco, lumber—the economy of the postwar city increasingly turned on a single cash crop. But what a cash crop it was.

Cotton was first shipped from the United States to Europe in 1784 and Charleston was its point of departure. By 1860, local cotton production exceeded two billion pounds a year. Plantations had become enormous, requiring the labor of many black slaves in order to be profitable.

Even before the emergence of the Cotton Kingdom, South Carolina had stood at the forefront of the pro-slavery movement. Indeed, its delegation to the Second Continental Congress, sparked by the young Edward Rutledge, prevented the inclusion of a passage in the Declaration of Independence that would have banned the "peculiar institution." During the 1830s and 1840s, when debates over slavery and states rights raged in the U.S. Congress, South Carolina's senator, John C. Calhoun, was a leading spokesman for the South.

(Above) During the Revolutionary War Col. William Moultrie, pictured here, and a few hundred Americans successfully defended Charleston Harbor against nine British men-of-war and 2,000 soldiers. The battle was America's first successful land-and-sea action during the conflict.

Thus, it was not surprising that South Carolina became the first state to secede from the Union in the wake of Abraham Lincoln's election as president. Three-and-a-half months later, on April 12, 1861, Charleston became the place where the Civil War began. The conflict started when a group of Confederates attacked a small contingent of federal forces bottled up at Fort Sumter, a partially completed fortress in the harbor. After some 34 hours of bombing, the Union troops, under the command of Maj. Robert Anderson, surrendered. Union forces returned to the city two years later, however, and treated its citizens to a siege that lasted 587 days.

A major round in the battle came in July 1863, when Union troops captured Battery Wagner on Morris Island. The assault was led by the 54th Massachusetts, an all-black regiment commanded by a white Bostonian named Robert Gould Shaw. Shaw and half of his regiment were killed in the engagement, but when the battery fell the Union troops had a suitable place from which to bombard the city. Shortly thereafter shells were landing in the very heart of Charleston, leading many of its inhabitants to flee the town. Finally, on February 18, 1865, Union troops took possession of what was left of the city.

When the war ended less than three months later, Charleston was in ruins. What had been a bustling city of some 40,000 people in 1860 was now little more than a ghost town. Its citizens were gone, its homes and commercial buildings were bombed out or burned, and its once-thriving shipping industry was in the hands of competitors elsewhere. As if all this weren't bad enough, a massive earthquake in August caused the city even further damage.

But Charleston rebuilt and in the intervening years has found renewed life, aided in part by the U.S. government, which established a first class navy yard there. Today more than 160 manufacturing and industrial concerns call Charleston home.

There are also thousands of historic structures in the city, the result of a remarkable historic preservation effort that dates back to the 1920s. There are abundant examples of Georgian, Neo-classical. Second Empire, and other architectural styles, and the buildings are set amid cobblestoned streets, and charming alleys, pungent with the fragrance of wisteria. Indeed, anyone looking for the gentility and charm of the Old South would be hard-pressed to find a better place than this.

(Left) St. Philip's Episcopal Church was established in 1670 but the present structure was constructed between 1835 and 1838. Buried in its graveyard are John C. Calhoun, vice-president of the United States and U.S. senator from South Carolina; Edward Rutledge, a signer of the Declaration of Independence; and Charles Pinckney, a signer of the U.S. Constitution.

(Below) The Aiken-Rhett Mansion was built around 1817 and enlarged in subsequent decades. Its original owner was South Carolina governor and railroad pioneer William Aiken. In 1864 it served as the headquarters for the Confederate general, Pierre T. Beauregard.

ST. AUGUSTINE

FLORIDA

(Above) In the heart of the Spanish Quarter is St. George Street where carefully restored structures and costumed interpreters take visitors back to the 1740s, when merchants, soldiers, and other settlers held their own against the British colonies to the north.

(Opposite) Pictured here is one of two marble lions that flank the city side of a bridge crossing the Matanzas River, the estuary where Pedro Menéndez de Avilés slaughtered more than a hundred French soldiers in 1565. Designed by J. E. Greiner and completed in 1926, the bridge is 1,583 feet long and reflects the Spanish Renaissance style architecture of the downtown area.

In 1884, when Henry Flagler first came to St. Augustine, Florida, the idea of turning the Sunshine State into a grand winter resort had simply not occurred to anyone. But it occurred to him. Indeed, the man who helped John D. Rockefeller establish Standard Oil was seized by the dream of making the oldest city in America a winter Newport. Thus inspired, he was determined to make his dream come true—even if he had to singlehandedly rebuild the city and personally supply it with all the municipal services a modern resort community required.

The town that so energized the father of modern Florida began as a Spanish bulwark against French Huguenots in September 1565. By that time, the hated Protestants had already established a colony in what is now Jacksonville. Hearing of this settlement, Philip II dispatched admiral Pedro Menéndez de Avilés to oust the French and to settle the land that Ponce de Leon had discovered and called *La Florida*, the flowery place. Menéndez named the outpost on the northeast coast St. Augustine for the patron saint of his hometown.

(Left) In 1565, Pedro Menéndez de Avilés was dispatched by Philip II of Spain to oust the French from *La Florida*. Not above slaughtering his enemies and blessed by favorable weather conditions, Menéndez accomplished his mission in less than three months.

(Below) The Gonzales-Alvarez House is a Spanish Colonial style structure that was begun in 1723. Known as the Oldest House, it originally served as the one-story home of an artilleryman named Gonzales. During the second Spanish period, it was owned by a baker named Geronimo Alvarez, whose family lived here until 1882.

Clearly the Spaniards, whose numbers included a hundred farmers, had come to stay. They had also come to fight, and shortly after arriving in the New World, Menéndez and his force of 500 marched the 40 miles to the French base and attacked. When the garrison fell, the Spaniards captured it and renamed it San Mateo. A week later St. Augustine greeted the arrival of more than a hundred French soldiers, whose ships had run aground in a storm. Left with little choice, they surrendered and the Spaniards, who could neither feed nor guard them, slaughtered them. A second group, including the French commander, Jean Ribault, met a similar fate shortly thereafter.

While the Spaniards had triumphed over their enemy in less than three months, they were barely able to hold their own against starvation, disease, and Indians. Salvation finally came in the form of badly needed supplies and a thousand men, courtesy of Philip II. Then in 1586 came a new threat—from Sir Francis Drake, who landed at the harbor with his huge fleet. Finding nothing worth sacking, the British adventurer contented himself with burning the town and destroying its gardens and orchards. Undaunted, the settlers rebuilt and by the beginning of the 17th century, St. Augustine had become what one visitor called a "noble and loyal city" of some 80 families.

But life in the colony remained terribly hard. Diseases, notably yellow fever, smallpox, and measles, took their toll,

and the colonists again faced famine and a lack of supplies. This time Spain, beset with problems of its own, turned an indifferent eye toward its colony. As if conditions were not bad enough, the Timucuan and Guale tribes revolted in what has become known as the "Great Rebellion."

Despite the difficulties, however, the town boasted some 700 residents by the 1660s, of whom about 300 were attached to the garrison. Perhaps the most significant event of the late 17th century was the erection of a stone fort, the Castillo de San Marcos, begun in 1672. This massive project inspired the construction of other buildings from coquina, a limestone formed of marine shells and coral, and tabby, a mixture of oyster shells, lime, and sand or gravel, introducing what some have called St. Augustine's Stone Age.

After 1702, when a new French-Spanish alliance threatened Great Britain, St. Augustine faced periodic threats from the English colonists to the north. The town was pillaged and burned during Queen Anne's War at the behest of Carolina governor, James Moore, and James Oglethorpe, the founder of Georgia, tried to capture the city in 1740 and again in 1743. Thereafter tensions eased, and the local merchants, despite Spanish regulations to the contrary, even established trade relations with their counterparts in New York and Charleston. But few in St. Augustine were prepared to become subjects of King George III when Britain acquired the colony after the French and Indian War. Although the new rulers were willing to let the Spaniards stay and even keep their Catholic faith, virtually all 3,000 of them chose to relocate to Cuba.

The first governor of what was called British East Florida was Col. James Grant, a former career soldier who used his friendships with colonists in South Carolina to bolster the new colony, offering free land and other inducements to those who would relocate. The development of the region was also fostered by a treaty with the Seminole Indians, by which the Native

(Left) Built between 1800 and 1810, the house pictured here belonged to a family named Genopoly. It is one of the oldest wooden buildings in the state of Florida, a unique surviving example of a small colonial frame residence. Although it is commonly called the Oldest Schoolhouse today, local historians say that there are no documents to prove that it was ever an educational facility.

(Below) Markland, as this Classic Revival style structure is called, was the home of Dr. Andrew Anderson, Sr. Built in 1893 of coquina block, the 2½ story house boasts a veranda with large Ionic columns. Today Markland is part of Flagler College.

The first governor of what was called British East Florida was Col. James Grant, a former career soldier who used his friendships with colonists in South Carolina to bolster the new colony, offering free land and other inducements to those who would relocate.

Americans relinquished much of their coastal lands.

Grant's tenure ended in May 1771, when illness forced his return to England. Thereafter discord emerged between some of the colonists who felt their rights as Englishmen were being violated by the absence of an elected legislature and by the new governor, Patrick Tonyn, who considered their demands seditious. Still, during the

Revolutionary War, the citizens of British East Florida remained loyal to the Crown. Although St. Augustine was never attacked, it became a haven for settlers fleeing the northern border area where forces fighting for England engaged in a series of raids against the rebels in Georgia and were themselves attacked in return. St. Augustine actually emerged from the war with an improved economy, as equipping and feeding the influx of British troops had created something of a boom. The citizens of East Florida even got their own legislature in 1779. But after the war Spain, which this time allied itself with the victor, regained its colony.

Again the residents of St. Augustine found themselves abandoning their homes in a mirror image of the circumstances that had confronted the Spanish settlers some 20 years earlier. Faced with life under a foreign power and the prospect of having to convert to Catholicism, only about 300 British residents chose to stay. Spain tried to induce its former colonists to return, but most of them preferred to remain where they were. New settlers immigrated directly from Spain and a group of Canary Islands farmers relocated to the colony, but residents also came from a wide range of other places—the United States, Italy, Greece, Switzer-

(Left) While a Spanish outpost, the Castillo de San Marcos withstood two British attacks. During the first, in 1702, a thousand townsfolk fled to the garrison for protection during a 50-day siege led by Carolina governor James Moore.

Begun in 1672 and completed 23 years later, the Castillo de San Marcos boasts walls 14 feet thick. After the United States acquired Spanish Florida in 1821, the name of the outpost was changed to Fort Marion, in honor of Revotionary War hero Francis Marion, known as the "Swamp Fox."

(Above) This is Hypolita Street, located in the old part of the city. The house seen at left, however, probably dates from about 1920. The grill on the windows, called a *reja*, gave a Spanish accent to the structure.

(Right) Pictured here is a guard house on the shore of St. Augustine during the period of British rule over East Florida, which lasted from 1763 to 1784.

(Left) The Cathedral of St. Augustine dates from 1787. The Spanish Colonial style structure is made of coquina, limestone formed of marine shells and coral. It was restored in 1887/88 and remodeled in 1965/66.

land, Germany, France, Scotland, and Ireland—turning St. Augustine into a very cosmopolitan community.

The second Spanish reign lasted 38 years. Then on July 10, 1821, Florida was ceded by treaty to the United States. Three years later, St. Augustine, which had been the capital of the colony for 250 years, was superseded by Tallahassee.

The U.S. had dispelled the Spanish presence but to win all of Florida, it still had to contend with the Seminoles, and in 1835, the Indians, led by Chief Philip, went on the warpath. What followed was America's longest and most expensive Indian War and the only one in which the navy was actively involved. There was no climactic battle, but by 1842 the Seminole conflict had largely dissipated.

It was during the 1840s also that Florida became a state and, of far less significance at the time, St. Augustine's Magnolia Hotel was opened. Thereafter visitors from the north, mostly the elderly and the infirm, began arriving to escape the winter's chill. But it took 40 more years and the vision of Henry Flagler to turn the town into a playground for the rich.

Deciding to build a hotel more splendid than anything seen in the state before, the peripatetic entrepreneur hired architects Thomas Hastings and John M. Carrere, the creators of the magnificent New York Public Library, and the result, the plush Spanish Renaissance hotel called the Ponce de Leon, opened in 1888 to wide acclaim. It was followed by another Flagler project, the Alcazar, designed for a slightly less affluent set.

In order to transport visitors to his American Riviera, Flagler built a bridge across the nearby St. Johns River, thereby gaining access to the railroad lines running north. He also purchased a railroad. And, in order to meet the needs of his guests, among whom were Rockefellers, Vanderbilts, and Whitneys, he acquired a laundry and a dairy, financed churches of different denominations, endowed a hospital, constructed a city administration building, and even built a baseball park. He also advanced the development or expansion of a host of city services—water, gas, fire prevention, and so forth. If ever a single individual transformed an entire community by the force of his will, it was Henry Flagler.

But the result was so successful that it quickly fostered the development of lands further south on the peninsula. Ormond Beach, Palm Beach, and finally Miami became the new tourist meccas. Even Flagler turned his atten-

(*Below*) Completed in 1888, the Hotel Ponce de Leon was the fulfillment of Henry Flagler's dream—to create the most magnificent hotel Florida had ever seen. Designed by New York architects Thomas Hastings and John Carrere, the Spanish Renaissance structure is now the home of Flagler College.

(*Right*) In his desire to create an American Riviera in St. Augustine, Flagler spared no expense, as the lavish plasterwork of the Hotel Ponce de Leon suggests.

(*Above*) The father of modern Florida was Henry Flagler, the man who, with John D. Rockefeller, helped establish Standard Oil. After visiting St. Augustine in 1883, he decided to turn the city into a grand resort, a winter Newport.

tion from St. Augustine in 1894, seeing in the virtually undeveloped Palm Beach a chance to build his dream city from scratch. St. Augustine hung on for a while, but the Great Depression spelled the end of its days as a winter playground.

Today it is the city's colorful past rather than its plush hotels or myriad recreational activities that draws tourists. In all more than 40 restored and reconstructed structures, including the impressive Castillo de San Marcos, beckon visitors to the Spanish Quarter, where costumed interpreters help them imagine what life was like in the first permanent European settlement in the United States.

(*Above*) Adjacent to the Whitehead Street lighthouse is a wood frame structure built in 1887. Typical of the kind of stations used by lighthouse keepers of the day, it is today a museum covering the history of lighthouses in the Florida keys.

(*Opposite*) Built in 1848, the lighthouse at 920 Whitehead Street ceased operation in 1969. Still in its original location, the 86-foot tower affords visitors an impressive vantage point from which to view the historic district.

The Spanish called it *Cayo Hueso*, meaning Bone Key, because the island was littered with the remains of the Calusas Indians, who had made their last stand there against the stronger, more aggressive Seminoles. Although the place came to be known by a number of other names—Thompson's Island, Allenton—the one that stuck is Key West, from the English pronunciation of the original Spanish designation.

The island was initially granted in 1815 to Juan Pablo Salas of St. Augustine as a reward for his services, notably as a member of the Royal Artillery Corps. Salas did nothing with the property, selling it in January 1822 to an American businessman from Mobile whom he had met in Havana, Cuba. By then Florida had been part of the United States for about six months.

The new owner, John W. Simonton, was eager to develop the island, whose deep harbor and strategic location between the Gulf of Mexico and the Atlantic Ocean seemed to offer significant commercial possibilities. He enlisted the aid of both the American consul and the American commercial agent in Havana, to whom he sold interests in the island. He also involved two other Mobile businessmen who, in turn, sold their shares to their employer, Pardon C. Greene. In addition, Simonton got his friends in Washington, D. C. to name Key West a port of entry and a wrecking depot and persuaded the navy to dispatch Lt. Matthew C. Perry, later responsible for opening Japan to the West, to survey the key, which Perry named Thompson's Island for then-secretary of the navy, Smith Thompson.

Simonton and his associates encouraged others to join them, offering homesteads to those who would help develop the island. Soon a community began to emerge, populated by some Spaniards from Florida but mostly by Americans from the North, notably New York and Connecticut, and the South, including Virginia and South Carolina. The settlers also included people of Anglo-Saxon and Celtic stock living in the British-owned Grand Bahama Islands. They were known as Conchs (pronounced *konks*) because in the early days of their settlement, when the Crown attempted to tax them, they had claimed they would rather eat conchs (mollusk-like shellfish) than meet the king's demands.

The people who settled in Key West were largely moneyed and refined. The homes they built, mostly of wood, a few of stone, often reflected the architecture of the places they left behind coupled with the influence of the Bahamas. Built to withstand high winds and a tropical climate, these structures were distinguished by wide porches, high-ceilinged interiors, and peaked roofs designed to catch rainwater for storage in cisterns. Many of

In 1822, shortly after Florida was acquired by the United States, Mobile businessman John W. Simonton purchased Key West from its Spanish owner whom he met in Havana, Cuba.

Typical of Key West's Bahamian style of architecture is the Audubon House, built in the 1840s by Capt. John H. Geiger, a salvager and the island's first harbor pilot. Now a house museum, the interior is furnished with 19th-century antiques and original engravings from *Birds of America* by John James Audubon, who visited the island in the 1830s.

them also boasted cupolas, known as "captain's walks" or "widow's walks," because they enabled their occupants to watch for returning ships or the wrecks of vessels that had run aground.

Although Key West was attracting some settlers in the early 1820s, there remained a principal barrier to the island's development—pirates. Since the 16th century, the likes of Edward Teach (better known as Blackbeard), Edward Law, and Captain Kidd had used the keys as a base from which to sack treasure-laden galleons returning to Spain from Mexico and South America. Finally, in 1823, the U.S. government dispatched Comm. David Porter to the island with instructions to secure the sea lanes for American trade and to make the place safe for the settlers. Using fast, shallow-draft boats, Porter and his Anti-Pirate Squadron, as it was called, made good their mission and by 1826 the "Brethren of the Coast" were no more. Porter liked Key West. He even established a naval station there, which he named Allenton, for an officer killed in the Caribbean by pirates. It appeared that the base's days were numbered, however, when President John Quincy Adams authorized the creation of a navy yard and

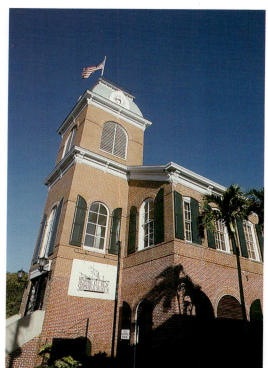

(Left) St. Paul's Episcopal Church is a soaring, white masonry structure erected in 1919 by architect G. L. Pfeiffer. It was the successor to three previous edifices on the site, each of which was destroyed by a hurricane. The interior features an organ with a hundred pipes crafted especially for the church.

(Top) Key West has always had a soft spot for artists and writers. Among its most celebrated 20th-century residents was novelist Ernest Hemingway, pictured here on the yacht *Pilar*.

(Above) Pictured here is the 1891 City Hall building designed by William Kerr. The first floor houses a Shipwreck Museum which features artifacts from the *Isaac Allerton*, which sank a mile off of Key West in 1854. Salvaging wrecks in the treacherous Florida waters was one of the island's principal sources of income.

depot near Pensacola. Then in 1829 Porter sent the secretary of the navy such a favorable report on what he called the "Gibraltar of the Gulf" that all talk of abandoning the base ceased.

By then the town had a population of more than 300. Incorporated in 1828, it even had a post office, with mail deliveries from Charleston scheduled monthly, although in fact the steamers were often several weeks or more behind schedule. Growth, however, was balanced by bouts with yellow fever, which took the life of the

The blue and white bell tower pictured here belongs to the African Methodist Episcopal Church on Whitehead Street. The first black house of worship in Key West, it was founded in 1865 by Bahamians Andrew Cornish and Catline Simmons and rebuilt 29 years later.

commander of the naval base and many of the men under him.

During the 1830s Key West blossomed into a successful maritime community. Not only were fishermen finding a welcome market for their catches in Havana, but congressional legislation in 1825 prohibited the salvaging of wrecked vessels in U.S. waters by non-American ships. This act prompted the development of Key West's highly profitable salvage industry, which saw some 20 good-sized vessels plying Florida's treacherous waters by 1855. That same year marked the

This closeup shows the alternating patterns of red and yellow brick with white and brown columns and trim that distinguish the First National Bank on the corner of Front and Duval streets. The triangular structure was financed in 1891 by a group of Cuban cigar manufacturers.

zenith of another local industry, salt gathering, which yielded 75,000 bushels in 1855. The source for this enterprise was the island's southeast coastline, where salt crystals up to a quarter-inch in size were deposited by retreating waves. Agricultural pursuits were not overlooked either. Pineapples and limes, for example, were lucrative island crops. Even today Key lime pie is a local institution.

But the island's most significant industry centered around the manufacture of cigars. The first factory opened in 1831 under the auspices of William H. Wall, a British shipwreck victim who also ran a print shop and owned interests in a salt manufacturing company. Before it burned down in 1859, Wall's "segar manufactory," as it was called in the *Key West Gazette*, had about 50 employees.

Key West has always had a soft spot for artists and writers—among its most celebrated 20th century residents have been playwright Tennessee Williams and novelist Ernest Hemingway. Thus it was with great pleasure that the locals welcomed John James Audubon in May 1832. While working on the island, the artist-naturalist discovered a new species of pigeon, which he named the Key West pigeon to thank, as he put it, "the generous inhabitants of the island, who honored me with their friendship."

Once a cabaret theater, this 1879 structure—
one of the island's first brick buildings—was
originally the warehouse for Wall & Co.
William H. Wall was a British shipwreck victim who opened the first cigar manufacturing
plant on the island.

(Below) This house in the West Indian Colonial Victorian style was originally the home of Thomas Osgood Otto, a pharmacist and artist. It is now a bed-and-breakfast, whose six guest rooms are decorated with period furniture.

(Above) It was Comm. David Porter, pictured here, who freed Key West of pirates between 1823 and 1826. Porter liked the island, referring to it as the "Gibraltar of the Gulf."

Key West, like most of Florida, was largely sympathetic to the South. On January 10, 1861, the state joined South Carolina and Mississippi in seceding from the Union. Three days later federal troops occupied the island's still unfinished Ft. Taylor, where they remained for the duration of the conflict. Some of the locals fled to friendlier cities, but the majority stayed where they were, simply tolerating the intruders. Key West saw no action during the war, but it was used as the berth for some 300 captured Confederate blockade-runners and it was the jumping-off place for Adm. David Farragut's 1862 attack upon New Orleans.

The years after the war saw a dramatic rise in Key West's cigar industry. The first impetus came from Samuel Seidenberg, a German émigré who owned a successful cigar manufacturing plant in New York. It was Seidenberg who realized that, by using Cuban tobacco and Cuban laborers in a plant with a climate like Cuba's but located in the United States, he could produce expensive clear Havanas at a fraction of the cost. It was a revolutionary idea and a tremendous success. Soon Seidenberg had competition from a Spanish manufacturer, Vincente Martínez Ybor, who had been forced to flee Havana in 1869 after his support for the Cuban independence movement led to an attempt on his life.

Prior to Ybor's arrival, Key West's Cuban population was minimal, but their numbers increased dramatically as their homeland's relationship with Spain worsened. Soon Key West was boasting Spanish-language newspapers and restaurants featuring Cuban cuisine.

Many of the newcomers joined the growing cigar manufacturing industry. By 1876, the island had 29 factories with 2,100 employees and was producing some 62 million cigars a year. It was so successful that it made the tiny island the 13th largest port in the United States and Key West the biggest— with a population of 25,000 by 1892—and wealthiest city in Florida.

But the island remained isolated from the U.S. mainland. Then in 1912, Henry Flagler, the father of modern Florida, brought his railroad empire to the keys, linking the islands to the mainland through a series of bridges that cost $50 million. Sadly, this tremendous feat of engineering was so damaged by a hurricane in 1935 that repairs were unfeasible and Key Westers again had to resort to water transport to reach the mainland. Finally the Overseas Highway was completed in 1938.

By then Key West's cigar industry had disintegrated, the victim of the rising popularity of cigarettes, competition from machine-made equivalents, the emergence of other cigarmaking centers, and the Depression in general. Today tourism is the island's leading source of income. When not enjoying the brilliant sunshine and the myriad recreational activities, tourists can lose themselves in an historic district that features some 3,000 structures, many of wood and sporting charming gingerbread trim.

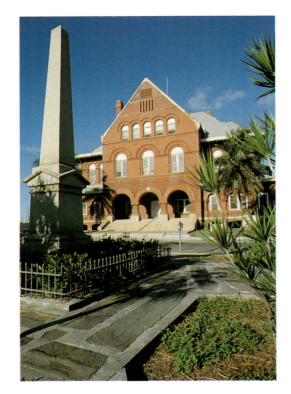

(Left) Monroe County, named for President James Monroe, was formed in 1823 with Key West as its seat. But the present county courthouse dates from 1890. Its architect was William Kerr, who also designed the island's Custom House/Post Office and the Old City Hall.

(Below) An elaborate wrought iron balustrade, reminiscent of New Orleans ornamentation, enlivens a structure in Mallory Square, where visitors gather for the nightly Key West ritual—applauding sunset.

(Left) An outstanding example of the Romanesque Revival style, Key West's Custom House/Post Office was designed by William Kerr and completed at a cost of more than $100,000 in 1891. Seven years later it played host to a U.S. court of inquiry investigating the sinking of the U.S.S. *Maine* in Havana harbor.

(Above) Looking at the Condé-Charlotte Museum House today, it is hard to believe that the residence originally served as the town jail. Built in 1824/25, it was converted to a private home around 1850.

(Opposite) Built in 1864, the Quigley House was home to one of Mobile's most prominent families from 1901 to 1963, when it was acquired by the city. It features a blend of architectural styles, including Italianate, Neoclassical, and Federal influences. The front facade is of high-quality red brick while lesser-grade materials appear elsewhere.

I f ever there were a city where cotton was king, it was Mobile, Alabama. "They buy cotton, sell cotton, eat cotton, drink cotton, and dream cotton," wrote a British visitor to the city in 1858. "It has made Mobile and all its citizens."

The downy white fiber may have *made* Mobile, but the town was founded many years earlier—in 1702—by a French-Canadian soldier named Jean-Baptiste Le Moyne, Sieur de Bienville. Only 20 years of age at the time, Bienville was a man of considerable energy and talent, who would go on to establish New Orleans 16 years later. He was principally attracted by the site's bay, which could support an adequate harbor. Moreover, it had an abundance of timber, it was well situated to check any southerly advances the British might make from their outposts in Carolina, and it joined a river system, the Alabama-Tombigbee, which gave access to the interior and the Indians who lived there. The settlement, which became the capital of the French colony of Louisiana, was called Mobile, from the name that the Indians had given the bay.

(Above) Mobile was founded in 1702 by a 20-year-old French-Canadian soldier named Jean-Baptiste Le Moyne, Sieur de Bienville, who would go on to establish New Orleans 16 years later.

During its early years, the French community and its inhabitants—who never exceeded more than a few hundred—struggled against poverty and disease. Supply ships from France were rare and yellow fever, which struck the community for the first time in 1704, was an annual occurrence. The fur trade was a principal source of commerce, as trappers from all over North America sent their kills to the colony. Trade with the Indians was also significant, but this was soon jeopardized by the settlers who, without European women, started taking up with Native American maidens. To remedy the situation, 20 women were dispatched from France in 1704.

In 1711, when persistent flooding made the settlement untenable, the community relocated 27 miles south to its present site. Seven years later, Biloxi became the capital of Louisiana (it was soon replaced by New Orleans), and in 1763 Mobile was ceded to the British as part of the treaty that ended the French and Indian War. British dominion over Mobile lasted until 1780, when the town was captured by Spanish forces from New Orleans. Operating at the behest of George Washington, they entered what was otherwise a foreign war between Britain and the fledgling United States because Spain was an ally of France, which had chosen to side with the Americans in the conflict.

The Spanish occupied Mobile until 1813, when America and Britain were again at war. This time Spain was siding with Great Britain, at least to the point of letting English ships rendezvous in Mobile Bay. Unwilling to accept this situation, President James Madison dispatched Gen. James Wilkinson and his forces to neutralize the town. In sore need of provisions, the Spanish garrison surrendered without a fight and thus America acquired its only territory during the conflict. Seven years later, Alabama became a state and Mobile was incorporated. It had a population of 809 at the time.

By 1820 Mobile had been an American city for seven years, but a Liverpool merchant described it as "an old Spanish town." It boasted 110 stores and warehouses, 240 homes, two churches, three hotels, and several public buildings. Its physical appearance was not impressive, with structures designed more for practical use than aesthetic merit. In the older parts of the city, the houses still tended toward the Creole style of architecture, which favored long, sloping roofs and front porches and were well suited to the town's hot, humid climate.

Mobile's residents, who numbered some 2,800 in 1822, included, according to one observer, "distant adventurers of every description." The city welcomed newcomers, especially those who showed an enterprising spirit. Sometimes, however, the fervor for business could go too far. Shopkeepers, for example, were known to attract customers by shouting at them as they

(Right) The Richards-D.A.R. House is a handsome townhouse in the Italianate style. Built in 1860, it was originally the home of Capt. Charles G. Richards of Maine who married the daughter of a local plantation owner. The house is located in the De Tonti Square Historic District, which lists 47 historic homes.

browsed at nearby enterprises.

Given the rough, almost frontier-like character of the town, it is not surprising that Mobile attracted many more men than women. Indeed, the ratio in the 1820s was about two to one. "The want of female society is sensibly felt in Mobile," acknowledged a local physician in 1823. Still, city leaders did what they could to bring culture and entertainment to the community. There were theatrical productions and horse races, and balls organized by the Masonic lodge.

As with so many towns, a devastating fire erupted to impede progress. In Mobile's case, the conflagration came in October 1827, when two-thirds of the business district went up in flames and property losses reached more than $1 million. In the aftermath, the town rebuilt, using brick instead of wood. It also organized six fire companies.

The town boomed in the 1830s, spurred by the growing cotton industry. During this decade Alabama produced about 100,000 bales of cotton. Within 30 years, the yield had tripled and most of it was being shipped all over the world through Mobile. By then cotton had made the town so successful that it boasted the third largest export trade in the nation, exceeded only by the exports of New York and New Orleans.

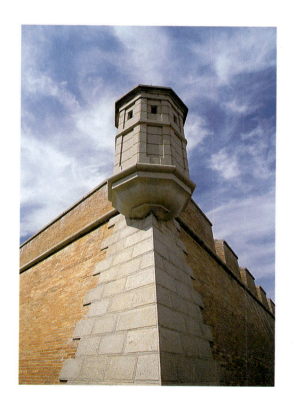

(Above) Although the creation of a fort on Dauphine Island at the entrance to Mobile Bay was recommended as early as 1713, when Mobile was the capital of the French colony of Louisiana, construction did not begin until 1818 and was not completed until the Civil War. Shortly thereafter, the outpost fell to the Union forces under Adm. David Farragut.

(Above) During the Battle of Mobile Bay in August 1864, the Confederate ironclad *Tennessee* stood alone against 17 Union ships. For two hours she was raked with broadsides and rammed at full speed until she finally surrendered.

(Left) Ft. Conde was erected in the early 1700s by Mobile's founder, Jean-Baptiste Le Moyne, Sieur de Bienville, after the settlement's original outpost—which was made of wood—became badly decayed. It was around this imposing brick structure that the present town grew. The outpost was renamed Ft. Charlotte after the British acquired the town.

If cotton brought great wealth to the community, it also exacted a high price. Mobile was completely reliant on the North for its marketing and banking needs and its imports, notably from New York, were staggering. Indeed by 1860 Mobile had the most unfavorable export-import balance of any port in the South.

Then came the Civil War. Although the local citizens dispatched dozens of companies of men to help fuel the Confederate military machine, their town remained untouched by the conflict until late July 1864, when a fleet of Union ships under the command of Adm. David Farragut arrived at the mouth of Mobile Bay, about 30 miles

south of town. Farragut's orders were to secure the Bay so that it could not continue to serve as a source of supply for Confederate forces in the West and to neutralize the cluster of outposts overlooking its waters. On August 5, he launched his attack against the numerically inferior Confederate naval forces. As his fleet, which included 14 wooden vessels and four ironclads, entered the channel, the *Tecumseh* hit a mine and sank. This sudden loss panicked the captain of the foremost ship. "Damn the torpedoes, full speed ahead," ordered Farragut, taking the lead in the assault himself. Most of the Confederate vessels were quickly subdued, leaving only the *Tennessee* to face the 17 Union ships. For two hours the lone ironclad was raked with broadsides and rammed at full speed until, finally, she surrendered.

Meanwhile, several gunboats from Farragut's fleet had been busy shelling Fort Powell. That night the outpost

(Above) If ever there were a city where cotton was king, it was Mobile, Alabama. "They buy cotton, sell cotton, eat cotton, drink cotton, and dream cotton," wrote a British visitor to the city in 1858. "It has made Mobile and all its citizens." Pictured here is an artist's sketch of a plantation near the city.

(Below) Begun in 1833, Oakleigh Mansion was designed in the Greek Revival style by its owner, James W. Roper, a Mobile merchant. Considered the preeminent residence in the Oakleigh Garden District, it is one of four historic house museums in the city.

was abandoned and its powder magazine discharged, reducing it to ruins. The two remaining posts, Fort Gaines and Fort Morgan, fell on August 7 and August 23 respectively.

The Battle of Mobile Bay was a stunning victory for the North. As for the city itself, it represented little threat once its ability to supply the South's forces was gone. Mobile finally capitulated on April 12, 1865, three days after Lee's surrender at Appomattox.

Mobile had been fortunate. Unlike many southern cities, it had not been destroyed by the war, but the town's luck ran out on May 25, 1865, when a town ordinance depot exploded. The 200 tons of powder and munitions stored inside generated a blast that demolished eight city blocks and killed hundreds of people.

Competition from the railroads and a severe shortage of capital kept Mobile from ever again realizing the levels of antebellum shipping activity. Nevertheless lumber exports were significant

The rooms in the Condé-Charlotte Museum House have been decorated to reflect various periods in Mobile's rich history. Pictured here is the 1763 English Council Chamber Room with its impressive Chippendale furnishings. Great Britain ruled Mobile from 1763 to 1780.

during the latter part of the 19th century. And World War II brought an explosion of activity, as thousands of people from the rural areas of Georgia, Mississippi, and, of course, Alabama sought work in the community's booming ship building industry.

(Above) The parlor in the Condé-Charlotte Museum House is a charming reflection of Mobile's antebellum period. In the years between 1830 and 1860, the town attained considerable wealth thanks to the growth of the cotton industry. By the time of the Civil War, Mobile was shipping nearly one million bales a year.

Today Mobile, with a population of around 200,000, has some 4,000 or so buildings on the National Register of Historic Places. They may be found in seven historic districts, each of which has its own unique character.

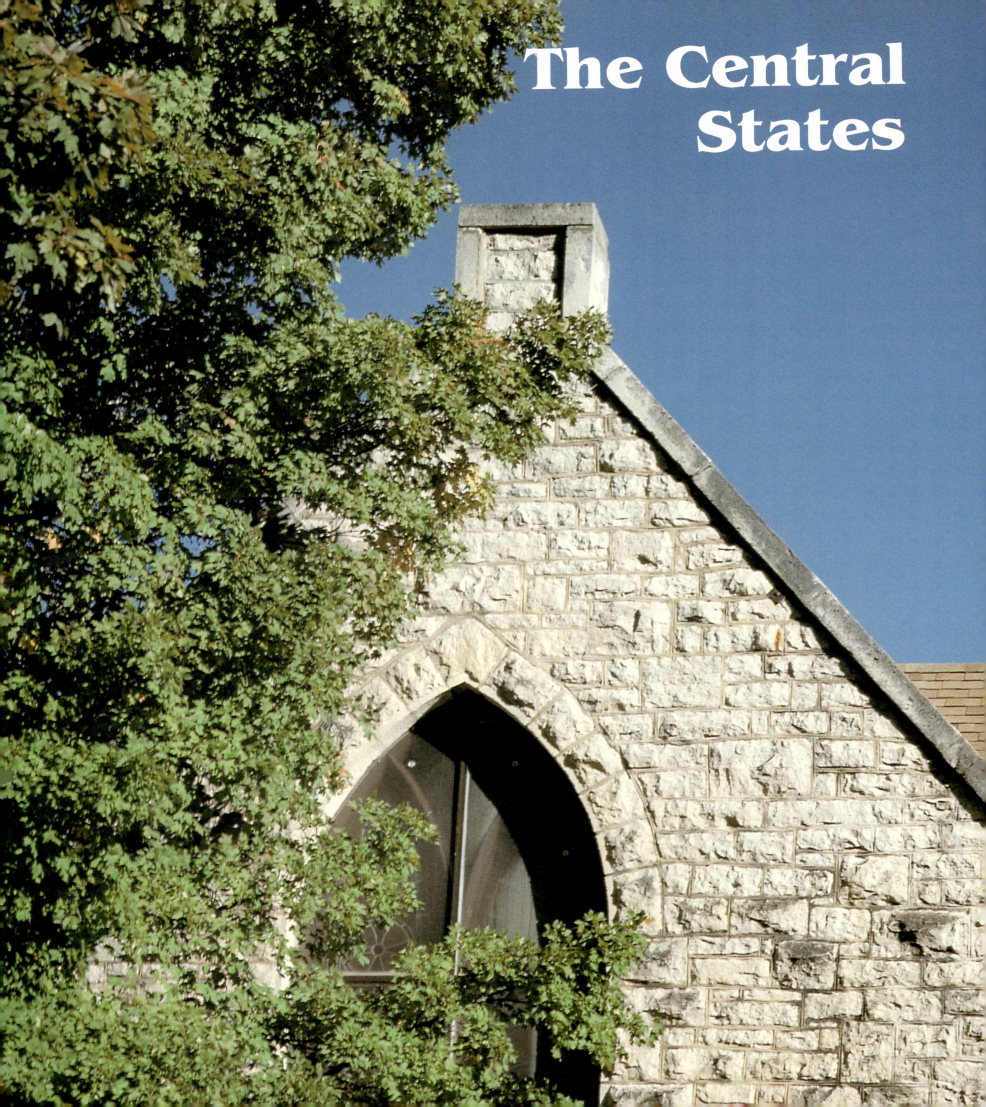

The Central
States

(*Above*) In 1969, more than 85 percent of Galena, Illinois was placed on the National Register of Historic Places, including all of Main and Bench streets. The downtown area is seen in this photo from the footbridge that crosses over the Galena River.

(*Opposite*) The Farmer's Home Hotel is a restored 1867 brick inn with seven guest rooms, two suites and a detatched cottage.

(*Previous pages*) The First Presbyterian Church, Eureka Springs, Arkansas.

A house! They had given him a house! Ulysses S. Grant must have been overwhelmed by the generosity of the citizens of Galena, Illinois. But then they were not strangers. He had lived among them before the war. Those were the dark years, when he had retreated to his father's leather goods store after he had failed at everything else he had tried. Now in August 1865, he was the hero of the nation and his former friends and neighbors were proud to claim him as one of their own.

The town that Grant called home was in the northwestern tip of the state. Unlike most of Illinois, which is prairie land, the town lies along the Galena River, a scant three miles from its confluence with the Mississippi, amid rugged bluffs, rocky ridges, and deep valleys. Long before the future president came to town, the community's signficant lead deposits made it the site of the first mineral rush in the nation. It was also a bustling river port, capable of competing successfully for trade with the likes of St. Louis and New Orleans.

Galena's fortunes began to rise in 1807, when Congress, recognizing the territory's mineral wealth, turned

(Left) Hezekiah H. Gear, a native of New England and New York, came to Galena Illinois to seek his fortune and, after years of trying, finally, discovered one of the most productive lead deposits in the region.

(Below) Galena, from the Latin for lead ore, was the site of America's first mineral rush. At the peak of the mining boom, the town was producing 80 percent of the nation's lead.

(Bottom) The Desoto House is an Italianate structure on Main Street, built in 1853 in anticipation of the Illinois Central Railroad's arrival in Galena. Recently renovated, the 55-room hotel is still open for business.

it into a federal mine district. Those who wished to mine or smelt lead could obtain leases from the government in exchange for 10 percent of the output. But Indian opposition prevented the granting of leases for 15 years.

Meanwhile, traders, seeing the potential of the area and its river locale, established posts along its bank. Among them was January's Point, founded in 1819 by Thomas H. January. The presence of these white outposts at last paved the way for prospectors and in 1822 the first mining lease was granted. In 1823, 16 years after Robert Fulton's *Clermont* made its first commercial voyage, the *Virginia* chugged into the area, becoming the first steamboat to ascend the upper Mississippi River. That marked the beginning of a tremendous increase in river traffic. By 1829, 75 steamboats and 38 keel boats had docked in Galena during the first six months alone, many of them eager to transport lead from the rapidly growing mine operations.

The town itself, named Galena from the Latin for lead ore, was established in 1826. "There is no civil law here," wrote smelter owner Horatio Newhall to his brother in 1827. "Not much lead was made here till last year. There were then four log buildings in Galena. Now there are one hundred and fifteen houses and stores in the place." The first miners in the area were primarily from Missouri, Kentucky, Tennessee, and southern Illinois. A notable exception was Hezekiah H. Gear, who hailed

from New England and New York. Like others of his ilk, Gear came to Illinois to seek his fame and fortune but for years success eluded him. Finally, however, he discovered one of the most productive lead deposits in the region and became rich overnight. He stayed in Galena, becoming one of the town's most prominent citizens and benefactors until his death in 1877.

Meanwhile, Galena continued to grow as a commercial center. As the steamboat became a major source of transport, Galena emerged as the prin-

Many American towns have statues of Ulysses S. Grant but none held the man himself so dear as the citizens of Galena, who knew him before he achieved greatness. A statue of the Civil War hero stands in the park named for him, which is across the river from the downtown area.

(Left) The Old General Store on Main Street is now a museum displaying goods that a small-town enterprise would have been likely to carry at the turn of the century. Almost all of the merchandise on exhibit is original to the period.

(Opposite) The Old Market House, built in 1845, was a focal point during Galena's bustling riverboat days. Here a variety of vendors plied their wares for the town's 16,000 residents while the second floor served as the jail and the meeting place for the chamber of commerce. Today, the Greek Revival structure is a state historic site housing an architectural exhibit.

(Below) The Dowling House is Galena's oldest residence constructed of native limestone. Built in 1826, it is furnished with primitive, early-19th-century pieces and features an extensive collection of local pottery.

cipal port between St. Paul, Minnesota and St. Louis, Missouri. Moreover, so many Galena citizens joined the ranks of steamboat owners and captains that they came to hold a virtual monopoly over trade on the upper Mississippi River.

One of those who came of age in the great steamboat era was Daniel Smith Harris, who arrived in town on a keel boat in 1823. He and his brother Robert were among the first men locally to embrace the new technology, building their own steamboat—the *Jo Daviess*—during the winter of 1832/33. One of their later crafts, the *Grey Eagle*, was recognized as the fastest boat on the river. Both men participated in races and in the years before the Civil War Daniel was probably the best-known and most persistent steamboat racer in the country.

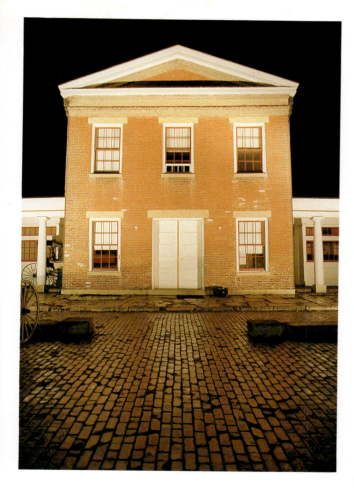

Galena flourished during the 1830s, 1840s, and early 1850s. The price of lead continued to rise, and the prospect of finding new mineral deposits persisted in drawing fortune-seekers to the area. Many of the prospectors earned little more than 25 cents a day, their dreams of great wealth going unfulfilled. But the town's large mine operators, supported by new, advanced methods of mining and smelting, did amass significant fortunes. Indeed, when Galena's mining boom peaked in 1845, the town was producing 80 percent of of the nation's lead. The business district boasted 34 grocery and provisions stores, 20 physicians, 13 tailors, 12 boot and shoe makers, eight hotels, five breweries, and two gunsmiths. Galena was becoming so respectable in fact that in 1841 a form of city government was established.

Much of the town's rich architectural heritage stems from the 1840s and 1850s, for as merchants and mine owners amassed their fortunes they sought homes and business establishments that reflected their new stations in life. A host of buildings in the Federal, Greek

Built in 1857, the Bellevedere Mansion is a 22-room residence in the Italianate style. Its original owner was J. Russel Jones, a steamboat magnate and U.S. ambassador to Belgium.

(*Above*) Pictured here is the leather goods store owned by the father of Ulysses S. Grant as it appeared shortly before the future president began working there.

(*Below*) Completed in 1845, this Greek Revival mansion was the home of Elihu Washburne, a highly successful attorney who became a U.S. congressman and later America's ambassador to France. He sold the house in 1882 because, in his opinion, Galena was "played out."

(*Above*) As the contemporary color photo shows, Main Street has changed little. After the town's economic decline, few residents could afford to dramatically alter their properties, much less tear them down and build new ones.

Revival, Italianate, and Gothic Revival styles were constructed during the town's boom days, and many of them are still standing.

But even as the town was flourishing, the seeds of its eventual demise were being sown. Believing that their future lay with the river, the otherwise farsighted city entrepreneurs decided not to provide a terminal for the Illinois Central railroad after Congress in 1851 authorized a line from Chicago to the Mississippi River. Consequently, Dubuque, Iowa became the terminus and reaped the benefits which Galena had eschewed. Worse, the river on which the town had staked its hopes was becoming difficult to navigate as

erosion from deforestation—the result of agricultural activities as well as the more obvious mine operations—caused the river basin to silt. The town's economy was further damaged by the Panic of 1857, which sent lead prices into a decline.

Then came the Civil War and more problems. Much of the available labor force joined the military and the town's access to the southern part of the Mississippi, notably the ports in St. Louis and New Orleans, was disrupted. Even the demand for lead, which increased with the need for arms and artillery, didn't help, for by then Galena's mines were nearly depleted.

It was during those years that the town's most famous citizen emerged. Born in Ohio and educated at the U.S. Military Academy, Ulysses S. Grant and his family had arrived in Galena in the spring of 1860. He had ended his military career six years earlier and had been unable to successfully establish himself in business since. At the outbreak of the war, he left his father's leather goods store, where he had been working alongside his younger brothers, and was commissioned a colonel of the 21st Illinois volunteer infantry regiment. On August 18, 1865, after four years of devastating conflict, he returned to Galena a four-star general, and took up residence in the two-story brick Italianate house that a group of local Republicans had given him. He

Galena boasts examples of a wide range of 19th-century architectural styles, several of which can be seen in the Main Street structures in this photo.

was elected president three years later and thereafter made only a few trips to Galena. In 1881, he purchased a house in New York City.

The end of the Civil War brought back not only Galena's favorite son but something of a resurgence in the town's economy. It continued to be the fertile agricultural center that it had always been and a new process for mining zinc gave something of a jolt to the mining industry. Hopes continued for a revival of the river trade, but these were largely unrealized. As late as 1892, construction was even begun on a lock and dam to ease the silting problem. Then came the Depression of 1893 and the town's economy collapsed. "Its streets became deserted, and the busy levee a place of echoes," wrote the *Galena Daily Gazette*.

But Galena's poor economy had one significant benefit—it prevented the destruction of many of the community's magnificent antebellum structures, because no one could afford to modernize or replace them. During the 1960s, this architectural heritage, combined with the natural beauty of the region, generated a new economic base—tourism. Today, Galena boasts no fewer than 40 guest houses and bed-and-breakfast inns—most of them in historic buildings—plus some 40 antique shops, art galleries, and artists' studios. A walking tour produced by the Galena-Jo Daviess County Historical Society & Museum includes 63 historic sites.

Perhaps gambling will be the basis for the town's next economic turn. The Casino Royale in Dubuque, Iowa, just 15 miles away, features games of chance, the Iowa legislature having legalized river gambling in 1990. Illinois has passed similar legislation but has yet to launch its own floating casino.

(Above) In 1865, a group of Galena citizens gave this Italianate structure to Civil War hero Ulysses S. Grant. Grant spent little time here, however, visiting Galena only occasionally after becoming president in 1868.

(Left) An engraving of Abraham Lincoln hangs above the fireplace in the library of the Grant home.

(*Above*) The Janis-Ziegler House dates from 1791 but features an Anglo-American roof truss which seems to have been added some 20 years later. In 1804, the original owner, Nicholas Janis, converted the house to an inn—which he called the Green Tree Inn. It later became a tobacco store under the proprietorship of Matthew Ziegler.

(*Opposite*) The Ste. Genevieve Catholic Church was built in the Gothic Revival style between 1876 and 1880. It replaced a log structure, which had been moved to the site in 1794, several years after the town had relocated to higher ground in the wake of a devastating flood.

Unlike its Canadian neighbor to the north, the United States has few tangible reminders of the once-pervasive French presence in the New World. There is New Orleans, of course. But the Creole and Spanish influences there, not to mention those of the Deep South, somewhat obscure the Crescent City's origins, as do the city's strong association with that most American of musical art forms, jazz. Perhaps the best place to trace the French influence on early American life is in the Show Me State of Missouri.

Ste. Genevieve was founded in 1735 by a group of French farmers who were experiencing diminished productivity on their lands in what is now Illinois. Deciding to try their luck on the nearby west bank of the Mississippi River, they named their new town for the patron saint of Paris, the capital city of their homeland.

The fertile river bottomlands around Ste. Genevieve—*le grand champ*—yielded the settlers bountiful harvests of corn, wheat, oats, barley, and other crops. In time, the river town's location also made it a profitable fur trading post and shipping center.

In 1810 artist-naturalist John James Audubon brought 300 barrels of whiskey and other trade goods to Ste. Genevieve. He returned to Kentucky shortly thereafter, but his partner, Ferdinand Rozier, stayed in town and became a prosperous merchant.

By 1752, the community had 23 residents. The homes of most of the villagers featured a type of construction known as *maison de poteaux en terre*, meaning that the structures were supported by posts sunk into the ground. They were typically one- or two-room residences made of logs and mortised with a mix of clay or mud and filler (twigs, animal hair, straw, and/or gravel). To protect the filler as well as to deflect the summer heat, the exterior walls were whitewashed. In addition, a number of houses featured a *galerie*, a wide porch that extended around all four sides of the structure. To demarcate one parcel of land from another, each property was fenced. These stockades were not intended to secure livestock, however. Cows, pigs, and horses were branded and allowed to roam freely through town.

The people of Ste. Genevieve maintained friendly relations with the principal tribes in the area, notably the Peorias and Kickapoos. Their associations were not so cordial with the Osage, however, who consistently harassed the citizens of Ste. Genevieve during the latter part of the 18th century. Some settlers were murdered, but these Indians contented themselves for the most part with stealing livestock and other valuables from the townsfolk.

The residents of Ste. Genevieve—like French colonists throughout the New World—were strongly reliant on their faith, Catholicism. But a church was not erected in town until 1752,

and for many years the community had no priest of its own. Rather, it was dependent on the clergymen of Kaskaskia, Illinois, who had to row their way upstream to Ste. Genevieve in what was a rather arduous journey of three or four miles. After King Louis XV recalled all of the Jesuits in the New World because of the Society of Jesus' strong support of the Pope, only one priest remained in the Ste. Genevieve area. His name was Sebastian Meurin, and he was permitted to stay only after he agreed to recognize the supreme authority of the Father Superior of the Capuchins in New Orleans.

Meurin was indeed an intrepid soul, who ministered to a congregation spread out over a thousand square miles. It is not hard to imagine how a never-ending round of baptisms, weddings, and funerals kept him on the go, with only a canoe and a horse to speed him along. Finally, in 1773, his entreaties for help yielded him an assistant, Pierre Gibault.

By the time Gibault arrived in Ste. Genevieve, the town was no longer under French control for, in 1763, Louis XV's defeat in the French and Indian War had brought an end to his empire in the New World. In the division of France's holdings, the lands east of the Mississippi River were ceded to Great Britain, but Ste. Genevieve and the other western lands went to Spain. This decision was fortunate for the citizens of Ste. Genevience, who much preferred to live under a Catholic nation with close family ties to the Bourbons than under France's major foe. Indeed, after the British took over Illinois, many French colonists living there moved west, swelling Ste. Genevieve's population to 600, a sixfold increase over what it had been at the end of the war. The Spanish continued to rule Ste. Genevieve, which otherwise remained a French community, until 1800, when it was returned to France by the Treaty of Ildefonso. The town then became part of the United States with the Louisiana Purchase in 1803.

Given their hatred of the British, it is not surprising that most of the citizens of Ste. Genevieve sided with the Americans during the Revolutionary War. Indeed, in July 1778, the town's priest, Father Gibault, was instrumental in helping a company of Kentuckians under George Rogers Clark take, without bloodshed, Kaskaskia and Vincennes, two British outposts on the east side of the Mississippi. When the British put a price on Gibault's head, Clark insured the cleric's safety.

(Left) In the foreground is the Felix Vallé House, a Federal style stone structure built in 1818. For many years it had been the home of Felix Vallé, a descendant of "Papa" François Vallé, who had served for many years under the Spanish as the town's civil and military commandant.

(Below) The Bolduc House, built for a wealthy, Canadian-born lead miner, planter, and merchant, included two rooms. As was customary among French colonial houses of the period, these chambers were used for a wide variety of purposes.

(Right) The Bolduc House on Main Street dates from the latter part of the 18th century. A stockade-type fence, such as the one in this photo, surrounded each individual lot and served to indicate property lines rather than to contain livestock.

(Above) This closeup of the Bolduc House porch shows the whitewashing that covered the exterior walls of most of the residences in town. The mixture was obtained by burning limestone, which was prevalent in the area.

In 1783, two years after the end of the Revolutionary War, a massive flood—possibly the most significant disaster of its kind in the history of the Mississippi Valley—virtually destroyed Ste. Genevieve. Thereafter the villagers moved to higher ground a mile or so up the river.

Wars and floods aside, Ste. Genevieve was rather a quiet place, whose citizens were not prone to violence. Several duels were recorded early in the 19th century, however. In one, which occurred in 1816, two

(Right) This photo of the Bequette-Ribault House clearly shows the preferred method of construction during Ste. Genevieve's early days. It was called *maison de poteaux en terre,* meaning that the structures were supported by posts sunk into the ground. The original owner of this house, Jean Baptiste Bequette, had been a voyageur, a miller, and a farmer.

(Below) The Felix Vallé House has been restored to the period when it was the home of merchant Felix Vallé and his wife, Odile Pratte. A portion of the house also served as Vallé's place of business, and his store has been authentically recreated.

opponents for the territorial legislature settled their differences at pistol point on the steps of the courthouse.

While the town's fortunes continued to reside primarily in agriculture and the river trade, it also boasted lead mining operations that dated back to 1723. By 1804, there were 10 working lead mines in the area, and by 1817 production was up to 800,000 pounds per year. A salt works on Saline Creek, several mills, and a pottery kiln also contributed to the local economy.

One of the mine operators was Connecticut-born Moses Austin, who came to Ste. Genevieve in 1796. After hard times hit the mines in 1818, Austin began to dream of establishing an American colony in the Mexican-owned province of Texas. He died in 1821, but his son Stephen brought his dream to fulfillment and today the capital of the Lone Star State bears his name. Another celebrated American whose fortunes were briefly tied to Ste. Genevieve was the artist-naturalist John James Audubon, who brought 300 barrels of whiskey and other trade goods to town in 1810. Shortly thereafter, Audubon returned to Kentucky, but his partner, Ferdinand Rozier, became a permanent resident of Ste. Genevieve. Even today, a town bank and department store are named for Rozier.

In 1817, seven years after Audubon's arrival in town, a steamboat, the *General Pike,* chugged its way up the Mississippi. But it bypassed Ste. Genevieve, stopping instead in St. Louis, the upstart community that had been established some 65 miles north of town in 1764. For decades, the two river communities had vied with one another for people and river trade, but St. Louis' proximity to the Missouri River gave it a decided advantage. As a consequence, it became the major jumping-off place for pioneers heading west, while Ste. Genevieve stagnated.

In the intervening years, Ste. Genevieve has experienced some notable changes. The town has welcomed several waves of German immi-

grants, who in time came to outnumber even the French residents. And new businesses have emerged, the most significant of which is the Mississippi Lime Company, which in the early years of the 20th century used the significant deposits of limestone west of town to become one of the nation's leading producers of lime and lime-based products. Today, the company employs roughly 25 percent of the town's work force.

But it is Ste. Genevieve's charm that is perhaps its most important asset. Recognizing this, the local residents—who number about 4,500 at present—have sought to "de-modernize" their historic district, installing old-fashioned street lights, adding other amenities, and erecting a new interpretive center for tourists. In all, there are more than 30 historic sites in the area, most of which can be reached on a walking tour.

(Top) Now a restaurant, the Price Brick Building is the oldest brick structure in town. It was built about 1804, shortly after the Louisiana Purchase, for John Price, one of the first Americans in Ste. Genevieve. For a number of years it served as the town courthouse.

(Below) Pictured here is a 20th-century artist's interpretation of life in Ste. Genevieve during the 18th century, when it was a bustling agricultural community, trading post, and shipping center on the Mississippi River.

(*Above*) Spring Street, seen here, was the site of a celebrated gun battle in 1922, in which six townsmen successfully stopped a band of Oklahoma outlaws from robbing the First National Bank. The event is still being re-enacted for tourists.

(*Opposite*) Built in the early 1890s, the plant pictured here was not only a source of ice but also a coal-fired supplier of energy. The Old Ice House—as it is now commonly known— was operated for years by the Southwestern Gas & Electric Company.

In spring 1879, Judge J. B. Saunders of Berryville, Arkansas was a sickly man. He was overweight and suffering from erysipelas, a skin disorder characterized by shiny red bumps and accompanied by high fevers and an overall feeling of achiness.

Fortunately the jurist's friend, Dr. Alvah Jackson, had just the cure—the healing waters of Basin Spring in the Ozark mountains of northwest Arkansas.

Jackson had long believed in the spring's medicinal properties. As far back as 1860, he had seen them work their magic on his son, who had complained of sore eyes after a hunting trip but was perfectly fine a day after bathing them in the waters. The doctor had also used the springs during the Civil War to minister to wounded soldiers and continued to prescribe them as a restorative to patients after the conflict.

Thus, it was natural for him to encourage Judge Saunders to build a cabin near Basin Spring and to bathe himself in the waters. Within a short time of Saunders' arrival in April 1879, the jurist was completely cured of his ailments.

Because Saunders was well respected, word of his miraculous recovery quickly spread and soon others seeking panaceas were encamped in the area, testing not only the Basin but also some of the dozens of other local springs. The arrival of so many newcomers sparked newspaper stories throughout the region and the coverage heightened the influx. Incredibly, by Independence Day there were some 600 to 800 people camped on the hills around the springs, most of whom were living in tents or crude shacks. One can only imagine what it was like in the encampment, where so many people bound together by physical discomforts were experiencing

relief—whether psychological or real—from their ailments. The quality of a revival meeting is the closest thing that comes to mind and indeed ministers soon arrived in the camp to preach the gospels on a daily basis.

It didn't take long for the health-seekers to use up whatever supplies they had brought with them. Soon a grocery store was established, as was a boardinghouse, and William Jackson, the doctor's son, opened a bathhouse. Among the first items to be manufactured were walking sticks, to help health-seekers negotiate the hilly terrain. In August, a road was fashioned in the hollow below the spring and the camp began to become a town. It took

as its name Eureka, from the Greek for "I have found it," and Springs for the healing waters that brought the people there.

In September, a dozen men—called the Committee of Twelve—were chosen to represent the interests of the people in the incorporation of the town. The first problem to be faced was that the health-seekers, while camping on lands available for homesteading, had not actually filed claims for ownership. I. N. Armstrong was hired to map building lots and streets, and anyone who paid the surveyor a dollar could become the proprietor of a lot. The land around each of the spas was preserved for public use, and, for those who couldn't partake of the waters personally, Missourian John Tibbs began bottling quantities and shipping them to the rest of the country.

Given an area of such rapid and significant growth, it is not surprising that several claimants came forward to challenge the health-seekers' rights to the land. Among them were three prominent sawmill operators, a group of land speculators who filed their claim in the Federal Land Office in Harrison, Arkansas, and an organization called the Blue Springs Mine Company, which sought mineral rights as well as land ownership. It took five years for the courts to decide that the residents of Eureka Springs indeed held title to the lands on which they lived.

On February 14, 1880, Eureka Springs was incorporated and two years later was declared a first-class city by the state. By then, it was the fourth largest urban center in Arkansas, with a population of some 5,000 citizens. The town had milliners, bakers, photographers, and, not surprisingly, 30 physicians. Indeed, the first medical society in the country was established here.

The town's growth was spurred in no small measure by the Eureka Springs Improvements Company under the leadership of Gen. Powell Clayton, a former Arkansas governor and U.S.

(Right) A crowd at the site of Sweet Spring in the summer of 1885 gives a hint of what the original encampment around Basin Spring must have looked like six years earlier when some 600 to 800 health-seekers filled the area.

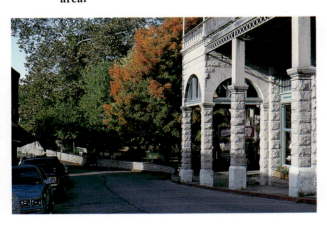

Famous Basin Spring, Eureka Springs, Ark.

(Right) This photo taken in 1910 shows the entrance to Basin Spring Park. Dominating the hillside above the greenery is the Southern Hotel, one of the town's first hostelries. It was demolished during the Depression after suffering extensive fire damage. The imposing structure at right is the Basin Park Hotel, which is still standing, as the contemporary photo above reveals.

senator. Among the Company's most noteworthy achievements was the establishment of the Eureka Springs railroad, which commenced operations in 1883. Six trains a day brought visitors to the resort, including, for the first time, members of the social elite, who made the Arkansas town a fashionable stopping point.

The population of Eureka Springs, which was relatively well educated for its time, enjoyed a wide range of cultural events. Literary societies met and a variety of musical entertainments and theatrical productions were offered. In summer, concerts were given daily in the park at Basin Spring and the opera house, established in 1880, played host to touring entertainers and dramatic companies. Public lands became parks and gardens, board—and later, stone—sidewalks lined the streets, and many of the houses featured fashionable ornamentation on their gables, rooftops, and porches. A quarry opened a few miles outside of town, and thereafter many of the new structures were made of limestone instead of wood. Gas street lamps were introduced in 1880 and in 1891 a streetcar system was launched, with mule teams pulling the cars. Perhaps as important as anything else, a waste disposal system was inaugurated in 1895, thereby endowing the town with a cleaner, healthier environment than many cities of comparable or greater size. In short, life in Eureka Springs was modern and convenient.

But almost unnoticed amid the growth and prosperity was a changing attitude toward health on the part of many Americans. The belief in natural healing waned as modern medicine and advances in surgical techniques brought relief from ailments deemed incurable only a few years before. The first sign that Eureka Springs' heyday was nearing its end came in July 1907, when the Citizens Bank went into receivership. Not only did many individual depositors lose their holdings, but also the myriad companies that bank president William M. Duncan

(Left) The Bath House of the Palace Hotel, the Ozarks' only surviving structure of its kind, still enables visitors to pamper themselves with massages, hydrotherapeutic baths, body wraps, and tanning sessions. In the early days, it made exclusive use of Harding Spring, one of the many healing springs in the area.

(Below) The Crescent Hotel, whose lobby is seen here, was built by skilled Irish-American stonemasons imported from St. Louis. Standing on the highest point above the city, it was called the "castle in the wilderness" when it opened in 1886.

had acquired upon the death of General Clayton were sold to various new owners. In the first decade of the 20th century, the town's population dropped to the point where only a bill passed by the state legislature enabled it to continue as a first-class city. Another blow came in 1922, when virtually everyone in Eureka Springs saw his or her investment in a locally inspired oil drilling operation go up in smoke when a fire destroyed all of the company's assets. That same year, a bit of the Old West came to town in the form of five Oklahoma outlaws who attempted to rob the First National Bank. Their efforts were foiled by six townsmen, who engaged the desperados in an old-fashioned gun battle on the town's main thoroughfare. Today locals still re-enact the event for visitors.

Although Eureka Springs' days as an elite health spa were over, the town experienced new life as a resort community during the 1920s and 1930s, when the widespread advent of the automobile inspired hoards of people to take to the road. Camp Leath, featuring an array of small rustic cabins, opened to vacationers in 1929 and was soon joined by numerous other such enterprises. Artists too began settling in the area, encouraged by a local entrepreneur who erected a series of small studios in—of all things—the side of a bridge, a 100-foot-long structure spanning a deep, woody hollow.

In the succeeding decades, Eureka Springs, like most communities, has continued to experience its ups and downs. Today, it draws people in part for its scenic beauty and its recreational activities, both of which were enhanced in the 1960s by a beautiful man-made lake created as part of the Beaver Dam project. But visitors come too to experience something of the Victorian Age, which is well represented by the many commercial and residential structures which have been restored and preserved here. So rich, in fact, is Eureka Springs' architectural heritage that in 1972 the entire corporate limits of the town were declared a historic district and placed on the National Register of Historic Sites in America. Thus, Little Switzerland—as Eureka Springs was once called—has fostered its own healing by becoming a living reminder of a bygone age.

(Top) Long before the health-seekers came to Basin Springs, Dr. Alvah Jackson had believed in the waters' medicinal properties. Not only had he seen them work their magic on his son's sore eyes in 1860, he had used them to minister to wounded soldiers during the Civil War. He is shown here with several townsfolk in 1879.

(Above) Eureka Springs' growth was spurred in no small measure by the Eureka Springs Improvements Company under the leadership of Gen. Powell Clayton, a former Arkansas governor and U.S. senator.

(Right) The steam-powered train pictured here is similar to the one which first arrived in town in 1883, linking Eureka Springs to the outside world and opening up the spa to the patronage of America's social elite. Today it carries tourists on short rides through the Ozarks.

(Above) As this closeup of a Spring Street building suggests, many of the structures erected in Eureka Springs during the late 19th century featured the kind of ornamentation that was fashionable during the Victorian Age.

(Above) The Rosalie House, constructed in 1883, is in private hands, but guided tours of the restored Victorian residence are offered year-round.

(Left) The Flatiron Building was constructed in 1880 at the junction of Spring and Center streets. Believed to be the first brick building in town, it was destroyed by fire and replaced by a second, nearly identical structure, which also went up in flames. The building seen here is a copy of the first two structures and was erected in 1987.

(*Above*) Between the 1830s and the outbreak of the Civil War, New Orleans became the busiest port in America, with an average of 10 steamboats in the harbor at any given time. Some of the steamers were so opulent and ornate that they became known as "floating wedding cakes." The steamship's golden age is recalled for visitors today by the *Creole Queen* (left), an authentic replica of a 19th-century paddlewheeler.

(*Opposite*) Quaint pastel-colored buildings with impressive wrought-iron filigree fill the Vieux Carré. Ironically most of the French structures in the old part of town were destroyed by fires in 1788 and 1794. What stands then in the French Quarter today dates mostly from the period of Spanish rule.

He was only a lad of 18 in 1699, when he and his older brother founded the vast New World colony called Louisiana. Now in 1718 he was a man of 37. Perhaps as Jean-Baptiste Le Moyne, Sieur de Bienville, stood on the deck of his ship looking out at the cold, uninviting water, he recalled how political discord within the community had forced his removal as governor six years earlier. Now he was returning with a chance to redeem himself. He was going to build a brand new city at the mouth of the mighty Mississippi.

The man who had given him the assignment was a Scottish financier of dubious reputation named John Law. With the support of Philippe, the Duke of Orleans and regent to the five-year-old king of France, Law had conceived a grand, moneymaking venture that called for the establishment of a great port in Louisiana. A host of nobles and merchants had invested in the enterprise, assured of fabulous riches. The new settlement—to be called New Orleans, for the regent—was even placed on French maps six months before it was built, the better to sell shares. But if cartographers had to guess at the city's placement, Bienville knew exactly where he wanted it to rise—on a

VIEW OF JACKSON SQUARE. NEW ORLEANS.

(Right) Dominating Jackson Square in the heart of the Vieux Carré is the imposing St. Louis Cathedral, completed in 1794. It was built on the site of two previous churches, the first destroyed by a hurricane and the second by fire. The present structure underwent significant remodeling in 1851, when a classical facade and the three steeples were added. It can be seen above in its pristine state in the chromlithograph of Jackson Sqauare rendered circa 1855.

Of course, Law's investors never realized a cent of profit. For a time the city's very future was in grave doubt, as visiting French engineers recommended that it be abandoned entirely. Once Bienville managed to have New Orleans named colonial capital in 1721, however, all such talk ceased. Then together with a brilliant young engineer, Adrien de Pauger, he began to build a more sensible, orderly community. De Pauger's master plan called for a town with 66 uniform squares facing the river. One of these, the Place d'Armes (now Jackson Square), was reserved for a parade ground with a church, a prison, and a barracks.

By November 1721, there were nearly 400 people in New Orleans. Food was in short supply, for the area's first major crops were indigo and tobacco. Finally Law enticed a group of German peasants to join the colony, and from their farms above the city came vegetables and dairy products to fill the local markets.

This most French of American cities became a Spanish possession in 1762, when King Louis XV presented it, along with much of the rest of Louisiana to Charles III of Spain. Curiously the citizens of New Orleans didn't find out about the transfer of power for nearly two years. When they did, they sent Jean Milhet, the richest merchant in the colony, to ask the king to reconsider. Louis never even met with him.

During Spain's administration, local land was granted to anyone who wished to farm it. This farsighted policy attracted, among others, about 5,000 French-Canadians, who became known as Cajuns. The years of Spanish rule also saw New Orleans devastated by two major fires. Thereafter new and better structures emerged. Ironically, the French Quarter as it appears today—with its charming, pastel-colored stucco structures—is not really French at all but Spanish.

On December 20, 1803, New Orleans again changed hands, this time becoming the crowning jewel of the Louisiana Purchase, by which President

piece of land overlooking what he called the most "beautiful crescent of the [Mississippi] river."

Bienville landed near Mobile on March 9, 1718, accompanied by a crew of 80. Most of them were convicts who had been given a choice of prison or participation in the New World venture. Many had chosen jail but were shipped to Louisiana anyway.

Building a city in what was effectively a swamp was not easy. The thoroughfares, made of dirt and shells, more often resembled canals than streets,

and many of the settlement's log structures rotted in the humidity. Others began to tilt in the marshy ground until they collapsed. But worse than the construction problems was the loneliness. "Send us some women," Bienville pleaded. In response, the regent dispatched 88 inmates from a female house of correction.

Criminals of both sexes continued to make up most of the community's population until the deportations finally ended.

(Below) The Garden District, settled mostly by Anglos after the Louisiana Purchase, features houses principally in the Neoclassical style with double rows of columns and elaborate wrought-iron ornamentation. The district's name derives from its carefully groomed gardens, many of which remain well kept to this day.

(Top) The Crescent City was named for Philippe, the Duke of Orleans and regent to the five-year-old king of France. It was he who made possible the grand scheme for a Louisiana port conceived by Scotsman John Law.

(Above) The 1850 House in the lower Pontalba Building in Jackson Square was home to several Creole families in the years before the Civil War. The enormous parlor, seen here in closeup, boasts an impressive display of mid-19th-century furniture, much of which was locally made.

Thomas Jefferson virtually doubled the size of the United States for a mere $15 million. Three years beforehand, in 1800, New Orleans had actually been returned to the French, given to then-emperor Napolean Bonaparte by the terms of the Treaty of San Ildefonso. Unfortunately for the citizens of New Orleans, the treaty was secret, and the terms were not announced until 20 days before the U.S. acquisition. Their dream of once again becoming a French city was finally realized, but it lasted less than a month.

Relations between the Creoles (American-born French men and women) and the Anglos were strained. The latter made English the city's official language, which infuriated the long-time residents, and the locals persevered with customs which perplexed the newcomers. Perhaps the most puzzling of these was the propensity for dueling. So popular was this method of settling disputes that on one Sunday in 1839, 10 affairs of honor were conducted at one site alone. Sometimes these deadly contests reached ridiculous extremes. In one instance, when a man from Maine was given his choice of weapons, he selected harpoons.

By the time New Orleans joined the United States, it was a city of some 8,000 citizens, described by one visitor as "a place of speculation, dissipation, debauchery, and revel, but not much for books." Louisiana achieved statehood in 1812 and three years later

(Left) The final resting place of voodoo queen Marie Laveau and the locale for the film *Easy Rider*, St. Louis Cemetery No. 1 was dedicated in 1788. Like all of the city's graveyards it features aboveground mausoleums because the land is so soggy, there is little alternative.

(Above) Samuel Hermann's Georgian style home was unlike any other structure in the French Quarter when it was built in 1831. A German-Jewish immigrant who made his fortune as a merchant, shipper, and moneylender, Hermann eventually sold the house to a Creole family named Grima, hence the home's present designation, the Hermann-Grima House.

(*Above*) Almost all of the early jazz greats—King Oliver, Jelly Roll Morton, Louis Armstrong—came from New Orleans. Indeed the city is known as the place where jazz was born. Today the great tradition lives on at world-renowned Preservation Hall in the French Quarter.

(*Right*) Now a bar, Lafitte's Blacksmith Shop was owned by the brother of the notorious pirate Jean Lafitte, known as the "Terror of the Gulf." Despite his running feud with Louisiana Governor William C. C. Claiborne, Lafitte fought alongside Andrew Jackson during the Battle of New Orleans in 1815.

(*Above*) Flanking St. Louis Cathedral in Jackson Square are the Cabildo and the Presbytère. The former, built in 1795, was where the American flag first flew over the city after the signing of the Louisiana Purchase in 1803. The latter, pictured here, is a contemporary of the Cabildo. Originally it housed clergymen from the cathedral; today it is part of the Louisiana State Museum.

(*Far left*) On January 8, 1815, Andrew Jackson of Tennessee won a stunning victory against a force of 7,000 British regulars at Chalmette Plantation, just south of New Orleans. With him were 500 Americans and the buccaneers of notorious pirate Jean Lafitte. Unknown to Jackson, however, the War of 1812 had ended 15 days earlier.

(*Left*) The Chalmette National Battlefield, about six miles outside of town, is the site of the celebrated Battle of New Orleans.

New Orleans became the site of one of the most famous battles in American history. At the time, the U.S. was at war with Great Britain and Andrew Jackson of Tennessee was given the task of defending the city and its environs. On January 8, 1815, he faced a force of 7,000 British regulars at Chalmette Plantation, just south of town. With him were 500 Americans and the buccaneers of notorious pirate Jean Lafitte, who sided with the Americans for reasons known only to him. Despite the overwhelming odds Old Hickory triumphed. Fighting behind solid defensive positions against columns of redcoats massed on an open plain, the Americans sustained only seven casualties while the British lost 2,000 soldiers. It was an impressive victory, if perhaps an unnecessary one. Unknown to Jackson, a peace treaty ending the War of 1812 had been signed 15 days earlier in Ghent, Belgium.

The decades following the Battle of New Orleans would see the city grow into one of the most successful ports in the nation, thanks to the advent of the steamboat and the cotton boom. The city's population reached 102,000 by 1840, making New Orleans the third largest city in the nation. Its levee stretched for three miles and by 1860 it was hosting 3,500 ships a year. Despite the difficulties of construction, which were not really solved until the modern age, the city boasted majestic hotels, plush gambling parlors, and theaters.

During these years, New Orleans continued to be a unique, exotic city. Part of its mystique derived from its large subculture of *gens de couleur libre*, free people of color, many of whom were the offspring of wealthy Creoles and their black concubines. The widespread belief in voodooism was also a distinguishing element. One of the city's most notable voodoo priests was a tall Senegalese named "Doctor John" Montaigne, who drew less on magic and more on a network of spies to blackmail many prominent members of the community.

New Orleans left the Union, along with the rest of Louisiana, on January 26, 1861. Although New Orleans was the largest city in the Confederacy, the South was rather cavalier about its defenses, and on April 25, 1862 it fell to the combined forces of Adm. David Farragut and Gen. Benjamin Butler. For the rest of the war, it was occupied by Union troops, and its citizens were both humiliated and infuriated by the high-handed tactics of the man they called "Beast" Butler.

When the war ended, New Orleans' economy was in shambles, its stores of cotton having been lost, its plantations destroyed, and its banks in ruins. By the end of Reconstruction, more than 30,000 people had left the city. So frustrated were its white citizens that they formed a militant order known as the White League, which in 1874 attempted to capture a cache of newly arrived federal weapons. It took several regiments of U.S. troops to end what became known as the Battle of Liberty Place.

The strife extended to politics as well, where southern whites dominated the Democratic party and blacks and northern carpetbaggers controlled the Republicans. In 1877, each party declared victory in the gubernatorial election and formed its own administration.

In the intervening decades Louisiana politics have often baffled the rest of the nation. For many years the state's affairs were dominated by the colorful, eccentric, and some would say dangerous, members of the Long family, beginning with Huey Long, who was elected governor in 1928 and U.S. senator four years later. Even in 1991 many across the country watched in confusion as a runoff gubernatorial election pitted Democrat Edwin Edwards, a former governor twice tried and acquitted of racketeering charges, against Republican David Duke, a former grand wizard of the Ku Klux Klan.

Today New Orleans is best known as the birthplace of jazz, the home of dining excellence, and the site of the greatest annual free show on earth, Mardi Gras. It continues to serve as a major port, although it has never again

(Top) During the early decades of the 19th century, the gentlemen of New Orleans had a penchant for settling disputes by the sword. One of the most popular places for these affairs of honor was Dueling Oaks at Allard Plantation, now City Park.

(Above) The Beauregard House, part of Chalmette National Historical Park, is a plantation house designed in the Neoclassical style by James Gallier, Sr. in the 1830s.

achieved its pre–Civil War zenith. But tourism is probably its greatest industry, with the French Quarter—the beloved Vieux Carré—offering an ambience that draws visitors the world over. An engineer once said "New Orleans was built in a place God never intended a city to be," but the Crescent City, the Big Easy, flourishes nonetheless.

(*Above*) Austin Street in the historic district features a rich variety of 19th-century structures, including the Excelsior House (the white building with the wrought-iron balcony) and, behind it, the red brick Jefferson Historic Society and Museum in what was formerly the federal courthouse and post office.

(*Opposite*) The Cumberland Presbyterian Church was founded in Jefferson in the late 1840s. Initially the congregation met in a small frame building, but in 1873 it moved to the substantial brick structure whose entrance is pictured here.

Legend has it that in the 1870s, the unscrupulous tycoon Jay Gould wanted to extend his Texas & Pacific railroad through Jefferson, Texas but the locals denied him access. Not one to take opposition lightly, Gould furiously cursed the community. "Grass will grow in your streets and bats will roost in your belfries," he predicted and then proceeded to build his railroad around the town, enabling Dallas to become the metropolis that Jefferson might have been. Whether Gould in fact cursed the community or not is subject to debate. There are those who maintain that he never even visited Jefferson. But in any event, the prophecy nearly came true.

The once-bustling river port in northeast Texas traces its origins to an 1835 treaty between the United States and the Caddo Indians whereby the Native Americans gave up all of their lands. After the Republic of Texas was formed the following year, that part of the Caddo acquisition claimed by the new republic was organized into the Red River District and opened to white settlement.

Among the district's earliest arrivals was Allen Urquhart, a surveyor from North Carolina. He obtained title to a 640-acre tract that lay on a bend of the Big

(Above) The House of the Seasons, built in 1872, reflects the transition period between the Neoclassical and Victorian styles. Its original owner was Benjamin H. Epperson, an attorney and close friend of Sam Houston. The northern end of the hotel, of frame construction, was built in the late 1850s by Captain William Perry, from New Hampshire. Perry was killed, through mistaken identity, by a Yankee soldier as he was standing on the corner near his home.

(Right) The most distinctive feature of the House of the Seasons is its cupola, pictured here. Each wall contains a different color of stained glass, representing winter, spring, summer, and autumn.

Cypress, a creek that met the Red River near Shreveport, Louisiana about a hundred miles away. From his experience as a surveyor, Urquhart believed that this acreage could form the basis for an excellent port city. A plan of the town named for the third president of the United States was drawn up on January 5, 1846; a genteel residential district was soon added. The appendage, which sprang from the large tract adjoining Urquhart's, became known as the "Alley Addition" for its owner, David N. Alley.

The first steamboat had arrived on the Big Cypress in late 1843 or early 1844, but those who settled in the new community realized that the creek would have to be freed of debris in order to make it generally accessible to river traffic. Soon a major clearance project was underway and by April 1845 Jefferson was fast becoming *the* place in East Texas for the disembarkation of new settlers and supplies. It also served as the shipping point for all the cotton grown within a 200-mile radius, an area that encompassed parts of Louisiana, Arkansas, and Texas. Business was so brisk that sometimes wagons bearing cotton were lined up for miles outside the Jefferson wharf, waiting for their cargoes to be weighed.

The dimensions of the Big Cypress and the Red River mandated the construction of narrow, shallow-water steamboats but a properly designed sternwheeler could transport a thousand bales of cotton along the Texas–Louisiana waters. Such conveyances came along after the development of regular commerce between Jefferson and other ports. The Kouns brothers of New Orleans, for example, christened a fleet of sternwheelers to ply the trade between their home port and that of the new Texas town.

As the port grew, so grew the city. In 1849 an English visitor counted "somewhat near sixty good houses and several large, well-supplied stores." Unlike most new towns, which were relatively unpolished, Jefferson—always more southern than western—bedecked itself in the latest fashions early on, not

One of the most celebrated events in Jefferson history occurred in 1877, when a beautiful visitor to the town, Diamond Bessie—Bessie Moore—was murdered. Although her husband, Abraham Rothchild, is widely believed to have perpetrated the crime, the murder officially remains unsolved.

just in architecture, where the Neoclassical style predominated, but in clothing and cuisine as well. Jefferson was a trading center, and its citizens were widely exposed to prevailing trends. Even that most sophisticated of cities, New Orleans, was a mere four or five days away by steamer and intercourse between the two communities was frequent.

The town was incorporated in 1850, and by the middle of the decade the population had risen to 1,800. In addition to the river trade, Jefferson boasted several burgeoning industries, including an iron foundry established in 1847 and a plow manufacturing company which started the following

(Below) In May 1961 Jefferson's grand hotel, the Excelsior House, built in 1858, was acquired by the Jessie Allen Wise Garden Club and lovingly restored. Many of the furnishings are original to the hostelry.

(Top) Portions of the grand Excelsior House date from the 1850s, when the hotel was owned by a New Hampshire character named William Perry. After his death, it changed hands and names several times until was acquired by Kate Wood in 1877. Among those who stayed here during the town's heyday were Ulysses S. Grant, Rutherford B. Hayes, William H. Vanderbilt, and Oscar Wilde.

(Above) The home of Williamson M. Freeman was built in the Neoclassic style on the owner's 1,000-acre plantation. Pictured here is the children's room, complete with rocking horse, dolls, and a teddy bear.

year. In 1847, the town also got its first local newspaper, the Jefferson *Democrat*. It was joined in 1848 by the *Jimplecute*, a sterling example of frontier journalism whose unusual name has confounded readers and historians alike for more than 140 years.

Although Jefferson was growing nicely during the 1850s, the town fathers recognized that progress would be greatly enhanced by a railroad link between their community and the prairies. Despite their best efforts, however, the railroad did not come to Jefferson until August 1860, when construction began on a tie-line between the town and Texarkana. Only five of the necessary 45 miles of track had been laid when the Civil War intervened.

Unlike other southern ports, Jefferson was never occupied by Union troops. Therefore, at the end of the conflict, the community's warehouses contained thousands of bales of cotton, which had been stored for the duration. With so many southern plantations and storage depots in ruins, the local traders could command high prices for their goods. Furthermore an influx of newcomers to Texas gave the local economy a mighty boost, inflating property values and dramatically expanding Jefferson's import-export capabilities.

Then in March 1868 a fire managed to do what the Civil War had not done. Flames spread over the central business district destroying some 50 buildings and causing more than $1 million worth of damage. But natural disasters were not the town's only problem. Occupied by federal troops during Reconstruction, the citizens of Jefferson rioted on July 4, 1868. Three months later George W. Smith, a champion of Negro rights, and three African-Americans were murdered. Twenty-four men were arrested for the crimes, and after a sensational trial, which took 71 days and involved the testimony of 176 witnesses, six of the defendants were found guilty on various counts and two were given life imprisonment.

By 1870, life in Jefferson had become more stable. The population had reached 4,190, making it the sixth largest city in the state, and only Galveston was more successful commercially. The local citizens had even resumed their efforts to attract a railroad. Finally, in 1873, they succeeded and the town was joined to a national network by the Texas & Pacific, the very line that Jay Gould would soon acquire.

Four years later, the talk was not about railroads but about the murder of Bessie Moore, a visitor to Jefferson. Known as Diamond Bessie for her collection of sparkling gems, this young, attractive woman was the paramour of Abraham Rothchild, a handsome jewelry salesman from Cincinnati, Ohio. When she became pregnant, a shameful condition for an unmarried woman in the 19th century, she insisted that he marry her. He reluctantly agreed, providing they tie the knot outside of his native state. By the time the couple reached Jefferson, Bessie had become Mrs. Rothchild. There, on a Sunday, they journeyed into the countryside for a picnic, but Rothchild returned to town alone, telling the locals that his wife was staying with friends. The next day he skipped town and a week or so later Bessie's body was found. The local sheriff tracked Rothchild to Cincinnati and brought him back for trial. Found guilty of his wife's murder, he appealed and was granted a new trial because of a technical error, and this time he was acquitted. While many believe that Rothchild was indeed the perpetrator of the crime that had all of Texas buzzing, the murder of Diamond Bessie officially remains unsolved.

By the time of Mrs. Rothchild's demise, the town of Jefferson was fading too. Dallas, which had become a major railroad center, was emerging as a serious commercial rival. Even worse, in November 1873, nitroglycerin removed the last of a massive natural obstruction on the Red River which for decades had impeded the flow of commercial traffic. It had only been a boon to Jefferson because it had backed up

(Above) The Hale House, built in the Greek Revival style between 1870 and 1880, was home for many years to May Belle Hale, a piano teacher and composer. Today this handsomely decorated residence, which features a number of antiques, serves as a boardinghouse, a role that it also played when Mrs. Hale and her husband lived there.

(Right) In the decades preceding and following the Civil War, Jefferson was one of the principal ports in Texas, whose commercial activity was exceeded only by that of Galveston. Pictured here is the G. W. Sentell, a sternwheeler developed for the river trade, at the Jefferson wharf on the Big Cypress.

water into and raised the level of the Big Cypress. With the obstruction gone, all of the towns on the river, most notably Shreveport, prospered. But Jefferson lost its backwater and, with that, much of its commerce.

While many in town hoped for a revival of the river trade, it was as a tourist attraction that Jefferson found new life. The renaissance began in 1950, when the community's vintage homes were opened to the public for a weekend billed as an Historic Pilgrimage. The result was so successful that it has became an annual event each May. In 1961, the lavish Excelsior House, built in 1858, was acquired by a local citizens' group and completely renovated. Finally, in 1971, the waterfront district was placed on the National Register of Historic Places, to be joined in 1983 by 49 other structures. Bed-and-breakfasts, some 40 antique stores, and restaurants featuring southern cuisine add to the ambience, making Jefferson today a must stop for those with an interest in America's great riverboat days.

(Above) Mile-long Main Street features a mixture of historic sites and contemporary structures. The street is wide enough to enable a man to turn around a wagon pulled by oxen.

(Opposite) Sunday Houses, such as the one seen here, were simple two-room dwellings, used by farmers and ranchers when they came to Fredericksburg for weekends.

May 1845 found Baron Ottfried Hans von Meusebach beset with problems. As commissioner-general for the Society for the Protection of German Immigrants in Texas, it was his job to see to the needs of the thousands of his countrymen who would soon be arriving in the Lone Star Republic. But the 33-year-old German nobleman was without adequate funds to house and feed his charges. Indeed, the organization that he represented was deeply in debt.

The Society for the Protection of German Immigrants in Texas was a body of some 20 noblemen seeking to build a string of settlements in the central part of Texas. But from their safe remove in Prussia the Society's members had failed to grasp the enormity of their mission. They were woefully underfinanced. Worse, the land grant that they had purchased for their colonial aspirations was extremely difficult to reach from Galveston, the settlers' point of disembarkation, and it was deep in hostile Commanche territory.

The Society's dreams of colonization had begun promisingly enough. Under Prince Carl of Solms-Braunfels, the Society's first commissioner-general, an initial group of settlers had established the town of New Braunfels on the banks of the Gaudalupe River in December 1844. But Prince Carl, unaware of the Society's shortage of funds, had allowed the debt to mount. By the time von Meusebach arrived to replace him in May 1845, a crisis point had been reached.

Blessed with a drive and determination that his predecessor had lacked, von Meusebach managed to renegotiate the Society's debt and borrow money so that he could deal with the newly arriving immigrants. To see them through the winter, he arranged for the erection of temporary barracks on the beach of the port city of Indianola. The facilities were hopelessly inadequate, however. Worse, an unusually wet winter and an infestation of mosquitos brought disease, including malaria, to many of the newcomers.

To alleviate the suffering, von Meusebach finally engaged a Houston transport company to carry his charges to New Braunfels, but before the journey could be launched, the Mexican War broke out and the services of the teamsters were commandeered by the U.S. army. Many of the Germans decided to make the journey on foot, but more than 200 died along the way. Those who survived brought malaria and other diseases with them and many of the citizens of New Braunfels perished as a consequence.

But better times lay ahead. Von Meusebach had found a site for a new permanent settlement, the lands of the Society's grant having been deemed uninhabitable. Located 80 miles northwest of New Braunfels in the valley of the Pernandeles River, the new site, named Fredericksburg for Prince Frederick of Prussia, was indeed well suited to settlement, with an abundance of water and plenty of wood and stone for building materials.

On May 8, 1846, the first wagon train of immigrants—120 men, women, and children—arrived. It had taken them an arduous 16 days to make the trek, accompanied by eight men from the Society's militia, but they were able to celebrate their arrival with fresh meat, as one of the soldiers had shot a bear on the banks of the Pernandeles. Each settler received two parcels of land, a lot measuring 100 feet by 200 feet in the newly laid out town and 10 acres in the surrounding countryside. An infantry company and a cavalry company were formed from the new community's able-bodied men.

In addition to cholera, which plagued the newcomers, the biggest threat to survival came from the Commanche, in whose territory Fredericksburg lay. But in March 1847 von Meusebach forged a treaty with the Indians, and thereafter relations between the Commanche and the Germans were primarily peaceful. Indeed, it would seem that this was the only Indian treaty in Texas history honored by both sides.

One month after the signing of the peace treaty, the Indians came to Fredericksburg to collect the $3,000 worth of presents that had been promised them as part of the settlement. The day was marked by the laying of the cornerstone of the Vereins Kirche (community church). Set in the middle of Main Street, this unique octagonal structure served as a house of worship for a number of denominations. It was also used as a schoolhouse, a community hall, and even a fortress.

(Right) St. Barnabas Episcopal Church provides an excellent example of German Fachwerk, which features rocks and mortar with wood supports.

(Below) St. Barnabas Church began as the home of wagoner Peter Walter, one of the original settlers of Fredericksburg. It didn't become a house of worship until 1954 when a descendent of the Walters sold it.

(Above) The Vereins Kirche, built in 1847, served not only as a church but also a school and community hall. Pictured here is the 1934/35 replica; the original was demolished in 1897.

(Far left) As commissioner-general for the Society for the Protection of German Immigrants in Texas, Baron Ottfried Hans von Meusebach was responsible for the wave of Germans immigrants arriving in the Lone Star State in the mid-1840s. Later, under the Anglicized name of John O. Meusebach, he served as a Texas state senator and a justice of the peace.

(Left) The seated woman in this photo, Louise Kordzik, was the first white child born in Fredericksburg—in 1848. She is seen here as a married woman with children of her own in about 1890.

(Right) The Old Jail, built in 1885, was the fourth such structure to be built in the county of which Fredericksburg is a part. It stands across the street from a modern facility, the county's sixth jail.

(Above) This porch is part of the Dangers house, which had been home in the mid-19th century to the Rev. Gottlieb Burchard Dangers, the town's second Protestant minister.

(Right) As this interior shows, the Adam Krieger House has been lovingly restored by the present owners, the Smith family, which acquired it in 1968.

In July 1847, von Meusebach, who continued to face shortages of funds as well as discord within the Society, resigned as commissioner-general. He stayed in Texas, however. Anglicizing his name to John O. Meusebach, he served as a state senator in the 1850s and later became a farmer and justice of the peace.

Von Meusebach's successor was Herman Speis, who promptly informed his charges in Fredericksburg that they could expect no further help from the Society. It was bankrupt. Discouraged perhaps, the colonists nonetheless determined to build their settlement on their own.

Ironically for a group that had kept so much to itself, the Germans benefited considerably from the presence of a Mormon community called Zodiac which sprang up four miles outside of town the year after Fredericksburg was founded. From these men and women of the land, the immigrants learned much about what crops to plant and when to plant them, information that they badly needed at the time. They also acquired at the Zodiac mill notched timbers for use in constructing their homes. No doubt they felt some regret when a devastating hurricane brought an end to the Mormon community five years later.

Also in 1847, the U.S. government began construction of a military installation, Fort Martin Scott, 2½ miles from town. Although the garrison was established to protect the colonists, the troopers sometimes brought more trouble than aid. On one occasion, for example, a soldier became drunk and quarrelsome in town and was killed by a bartender. The next day, a group of the deceased's comrades burned down the saloon and the adjacent store.

Despite the hardships, new wagon trains of German colonists continued to join the first settlers in Fredericksburg. By mid-1847, the population had reached nearly 1,000. The town boasted 15 stores, several large cornfields, and a wagon road that led to Austin.

In what seems to have been a unique practice, the local farmers and ranchers used their town lots to erect weekend homes. They would arrive in town on Saturday, shop, go to the theater or a dance perhaps, attend church, enjoy a sumptuous Sunday dinner, visit with friends and neighbors, and then return to their homesteads in time to start a new work week. Initially, these homes—called Sunday Houses—were crude, single-room huts, but in later years they were replaced by log and stone structures, usually consisting of two rooms, one on top of the other and connected by an outside stairway.

The Civil War was a difficult time for Fredericksburg, as the majority of its citizens were loyal to the Union and Texas was part of the Confederacy. The area fell under the jurisdiction of Col. James Duff, who brought a reign of terror to the German-Americans. In one notorious incident, Duff tracked down a group of 79 young men camped along the Nueces River in an attempt to go north and join the Union army by way of Mexico. Only 17 survived the onslaught and of these, 14 were hunted down and murdered by Duff's men. In the aftermath of the bloody Nueces Massacre, the colonel was recalled and mustered out of the Confederate army.

Undoubtedly Fredericksburg's most famous native son was Adm. Chester W. Nimitz, the commander of the Pacific Fleet during World War II. Nimitz' paternal grandfather, Charles W. Nimitz, had been the owner of the Nimitz Hotel, which had once been the only real hostelry between El Paso and San Diego, California. Built in 1852, the hotel had been famous for its German cuisine, casino-theater, and clean beds.

Along with the Nimitz Hotel, which has been restored to its 1880s glory, Fredericksburg boasts more than 80 sites in an historic district that vividly reminds visitors of the contributions German-Americans made to the settlement of Texas. A walking tour is available from the Convention and Visitors Bureau. The boyhood home of the Hill Country's favorite son, Lyndon B. Johnson, is about 30 miles away.

(*Below*) Fredericksburg's most famous native son was Adm. Chester W. Nimitz, the commander of the Pacific Fleet during World War II.

(*Above*) Seen here is what is known as the Oldest Room of the Nimitz Hotel. Restoration of the interior's structure, which was modernized in the 1920s, is continuing.

(*Left*) The Nimitz Hotel dates back to 1852 but its distinctive steamboat shape came with an 1880s addition. It was owned by Charles W. Nimitz, grandfather of the celebrated World War II admiral.

(*Above*) The residential areas along North Buckeye, 3rd, and North Vine streets feature a number of imposing homes from the late 19th and early 20th centuries. Among them is the Seelye Mansion at 1105 North Buckeye, built in the Georgian style in 1905.

(*Opposite*) Seen here is the Lebold-Vahsholtz Mansion at 106 North Vine Street, a stone Italianate structure built in 1880. Its original owner was C. H. Lebold, a banker, entrepreneur, and mayor of Abilene.

The scenario has been replayed in countless movie and TV westerns, as well as in the paintings of Frederic Remington and Charles M. Russell: a group of cheering cowboys come galloping into town, their raised pistols blasting away and the locals dashing for cover in their wake. A couple of cowboys get so carried away that they ride their horses right into one of the local establishments. Before long the rowdies have taken over the town. They are bathing in the hotel, fondling women in the brothels, bedecking themselves in fancy gear in the emporium, and, of course, drinking and gambling. Invariably one of them gets drunk and picks a fight with one of the townsfolk. Words are exchanged, the combatants go for their guns, and, when the smoke clears, the local lies dead on the floor. After a few days the cowboys leave, their money and energy spent, and the townsfolk breathe a collective sigh of relief.

There is one place above all others that gave rise to this scenario. It was the first cowtown and everything that occurred subsequently in other places happened here first. Its name was Abilene.

Before the cows came, the community in east central Kansas was just a dusty village with about 20 houses, a hotel, a blacksmith's shop, a brickmaker's shop, and a few stores. The area had been settled in 1858 by Timothy F. Hersey and his family, who were attracted by its fertile land, ample water supply, and proximity to a major east-west passage, which became in time the route of the Butterfield Overland Stage. To pick a name for their new home, Mrs. Hersey opened the Bible at random, came upon the third chapter of Luke, and spied in the first verse the name Abilene, meaning City of the Plains.

The town was laid out in 1860, but it wasn't until 1866 and the arrival of the Kansas Pacific railroad that the community began to blossom. With the Civil War behind them and transportation to the area relatively easy, many people from back East as well as new immigrants to the Promised Land sought to build fresh lives for themselves and their families on the Plains. In this, they were encouraged by the Homestead Act of 1862, which offered free land to those willing to improve it.

The man responsible for turning this peaceful, growing town of neat frame houses into the Babylon of the West was Joseph G. McCoy, a young, ambitious livestock dealer from Illinois. Inspired by reports of millions of longhorn cattle grazing in Texas, he saw in the advancing railroad an economic means of bringing the herds to market. He was particularly attracted to Kansas as a place where, as he later put it, "the southern drover and northern buyer could meet upon an equal footing . . . ." A train trip across the state convinced him that Abilene was the right place to set up shop.

Purchasing 230 acres, he began erecting pens capable of holding up to 3,000 head of cattle. He also installed a 10-ton scale that could weigh 200 cows at once and built the kind of support

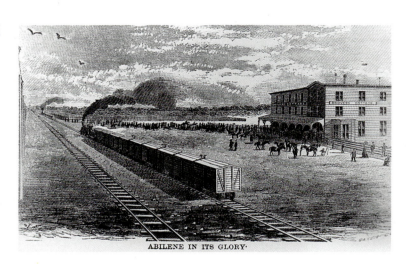

ABILENE IN ITS GLORY.

(Right) This print entitled "Abilene in its Glory" shows the railhead that made the community the first of the celebrated Kansas cowtowns. Estimates vary but between 1867 and 1871 no less than one million head of beef were shipped east from here. The Drovers' Cottage, an 80-room hotel built for the cattlemen by Joseph McCoy, is depicted in the background.

(Above) The first marshal of Abilene was Thomas James Smith, a former New York policeman and railroad worker who sought to avoid gunplay in town. After five very impressive months in office, he was beheaded while trying to arrest a farmer.

(Left) It was with the coming of the Kansas Pacific railroad in 1866 that Abilene began to blossom, emerging as the first Kansas cowtown a year later. The station pictured here, however, dates from the 1930s. It is still in use, serving the Sante Fe railroad, which is particularly appropriate given its Spanish Mission Revival style.

structures that his enterprise would require—a livery stable, a barn, an office, and an 80-room hotel called the Drovers' Cottage. He also secured the support of the governor of the state and an agreement from the railroad, whereby the cattle would be shipped to the stockyards in St. Louis and Chicago at $5 a carload.

Then all he had to do was let the Texas ranchers know that Abilene was open for business. To that end, he sent out flyers and placed ads in Lone Star State newspapers. He also dispatched a friend by the name of W. W. Sugg to ride south and intercept the drovers already headed for Missouri. Eager to shave hundreds of miles off the trek to the railhead, they turned north. One day in August 1867 the cows began to arrive. By the end of that first season more than a thousand railroad cars filled with cattle had shipped out of Abilene.

The following season started off even better. Then McCoy's buyers began hearing rumors about a deadly fever infecting the herds. Before his burgeoning enterprise could collapse, the livestock dealer hit upon an ingenious idea—a Wild West Show complete with cowboys, cattle, and horses, which he shipped off to St. Louis and Chicago. There, displays of the plainsman's art soon assuaged fears about the diseased stock. As a capper, McCoy convinced his customers to join him in Kansas for a genuine buffalo hunt. They went, and afterward he simply rerouted them by the stockyards. By then the fever had subsided and business proceeded as before. The following year, 1869, saw 150,000 head of cattle fill McCoy's holding pens.

Driving upwards of 25,000 obstreperous beasts on a journey that took about three months was mind-numbing work. Most of the herds followed the 600-mile trail from San Antonio, Texas which had been pioneered by a Scottish-Cherokee trader named Jesse Chisholm. When the cowboys reached Abilene—there were usually about 40 or 50 per drive—they were in dire need

(*Above*) In this print, Frederic Remington effectively captured the reckless energy of the cowboys coming into Abilene at the end of a long cattle drive.

(*Left*) For eight months, James Butler Hickok—better known as Wild Bill—was marshal of Abilene. A loner who loved gambling more than anything else, Hickok left town after he accidently killed a fellow law enforcement officer during a melée with some cowboys.

of a good time, and since the end of the trail meant payday they certainly had the wherewithal. To accommodate them, a host of new businesses rose up in Abilene. There was the Alamo, one of about eight saloons. It was a classic western watering hole with a long bar, paintings of fleshly nudes on the walls, and brass lighting fixtures. There was Jake Karatofsky's Great Western Store, which featured boots, hats, and "gents

furnishing goods" at highly inflated prices. And about half a mile from the center of town there was a red-light district that the locals called the Devil's Addition. About the only thing that the town lacked—not that the cowboys cared—was any form of law enforcement. "Murder, lust, highway robbery and whores run the city by day and night," lamented one newspaper editor in the florid language of the day.

(*Left*) Now a restaurant, this Victorian mansion in the Second Empire style has been restored to its appearance in 1885, when it was the home of banker Thomas Kirby. It stands on the site of what had been Joseph McCoy's home.

(Left) As this intimate corner suggests, the Seelye mansion has been carefully furnished by its present owners in the Georgian style. Placed on the National Register of Historic Places in 1986, it is open to the public for tours.

(Above) The man responsible for turning Abilene into a raucous cowtown was Joseph G. McCoy, a young, ambitious livestock dealer from Illinois.

(Right) The former home of Dr. and Mrs A. B. Seelye features, among other things, 11 bedrooms, a bowling alley, and a ballroom. Seelye, who made his money developing patent medicines, maintained a laboratory in Abilene. He also operated a local opera house.

Pictured here is St. Andrews Catholic Church on South Buckeye. Built in 1916 in the Romanesque style, it is still used today as a house of worship.

The corner building on 2nd Street was originally occupied in 1886 by Highland Southworth, an attorney and land agent. It later became the home of Etherington & Co. Real Estate. The sign reading "Straight Talk Real Estate" was put up as a novelty by a subsequent occupant.

Finally in 1869 the town was incorporated, and the locals, whose numbers had been steadily increasing—one real estate agent had been selling farms at the rate of about 10 to 15 a day—decided that the time had come to bring law and order to their community. In an era when a badge was often the only thing that distinguished a lawman from the outlaws in his charge, the first marshal of Abilene, Thomas James Smith, was a genuine find. A former New York policeman and railroad worker, Smith was a handsome redhead with a quiet manner. The first order of business, he decided, was to prohibit anyone from carrying a firearm in town.

Hearing about the new prohibition, a cowboy named Wyoming Frank bet his friends that he could best the marshal. It was a Sunday when he rode into town wearing a gun. When Smith asked for his weapon, Frank scoffed, but he backed his way from the street into a saloon with the marshal advancing toward him. Inside, Smith punched him down, took away his gun, and told him to leave town. Which Wyoming Frank meekly did. The onlookers were so impressed that they tendered their weapons on the spot.

Five months later, in November 1870, Smith went after a farmer who was wanted for murder. He found his quarry, but a friend of the accused grabbed an ax and decapitated the marshal. It was a sad day indeed when this dedicated law enforcement officer passed on.

Abilene's second marshal was the former sheriff of Hays City, Kansas, James Butler Hickok. Born in Homer, Illinois in 1837, James became known at an early age as Wild Bill to distinguish him from his brother Lorenzo, who was called—naturally—Tame Bill. A former scout and guide, Hickok was a notorious gunman who once claimed to have killed more than a hundred men "all for good reasons." Above all, Wild Bill loved gambling, and, after his appointment as marshal, he made the Alamo Saloon his headquarters. For eight months he preserved the peace in Abilene, keeping to himself most of the time. Then, on the night of October 5, 1871, there was a fracas caused by some cowboys from Texas. Hickok shot their leader, then fired again when he heard someone approaching him. In his haste, he had killed a friend and fellow law enforcement officer. Filled with remorse, Wild Bill got drunk and ran all the cowboys out of town. For the law-abiding folk of Abilene, this incident was the last straw. On December 13, they fired Hickok and thereafter published a notice in several Texas newspapers advising the cattlemen that their presence was no longer welcome in Abilene.

As quickly as it had come, the cattle boom ended. Wild Bill drifted off to a stint in a melodrama with his friend, Buffalo Bill Cody, and was killed four years later in Deadwood, South Dakota by a former buffalo hunter named Jack McCall. Other cowtowns—Ellsworth, Wichita, and Dodge City—arose to take Abilene's place. And Abilene settled into the quiet respectability that it sought. Even Joe McCoy moved on. "Business is not as brisk as it used to be during the cattle season," noted the local paper in 1872, "but the citizens have the satisfaction of knowing that 'hell is more than 60 miles away'."

Today Abilene is a prosperous city of some 6,500 citizens. Known as one of the "biggest little cities" in the Midwest, it is also among the richest and most diversified agricultural communities in Kansas. In addition to visiting the real thing, Old West aficionados might want to stop by Old Abilene Town, a re-creation of the community during Wild Bill's day.

(Left) Although he was born in Dennison, Texas, Dwight D. Eisenhower grew up in this white frame house in Abilene. The home had been occupied by members of his family since the 1890s.

(Below) Today the Eisenhower home is a museum covering the life of the man who served as supreme allied commander during World War II and president of the United States.

(*Above*) This two-story structure, built in 1859, is named for its architect, Abbot Gates, who also designed a number of downtown buildings. It is believed to be the first brick house in Brownville, which would also make it the first brick house in the state since the latter's first brickworks were here in town.

(*Opposite*) In its heyday the opera house on Main Street played host to traveling shows of all kinds, as well as concerts, lectures, local theatrical productions, dances, and box suppers. Today it continues to serve as a community gathering place.

According to a local 1867 newspaper, Brownville was "certainly the liveliest, thrivingest, grow-biggest and fastest town of its size on the Missouri." Local boosterism and the use of the English language aside, the writer was not mistaken. Indeed, this prosperous community seemed to incorporate all the values that defined America itself—vigor, enterprise, self-confidence—which made Brownville's fall all the more surprising. If ever a town seemed born to succeed, it was this one.

Brownville's origins can be traced to May 1854, when Congress passed the Kansas-Nebraska Act. Not only did this legislation open up vast new lands for settlement, it gave the residents—in what amounted to a repeal of the Missouri Compromise of 1820—the right to decide whether their territories would be slave or free. A scant three months later, a short, young dynamo named Richard Brown decided to leave his home in Oregon, Missouri and try his luck in the lands across the Missouri River. On August 29, 1854, he laid the foundation for his cabin, which became the first house in one of the first towns in Nebraska.

(*Above*) Brownville was named for the Tennessee-born Missourian Richard Brown who became one of the first settlers in the newly opened Nebraska Territory in 1854. Five years later he left the community to try his luck in Texas. He returned in 1860 but left again during the Civil War, no doubt because of his pro-slavery stance.

(*Right*) This two-story mansion in what is called the Hudson River Bracketed style was completed about 1872. Its owner was Robert Muir, a rather energetic gentleman who at one time or another ran a sawmill and flour mill, owned a ferry boat, sold real estate, was a publisher of the *Nebraska Advertiser*, and ran for state governor on the Prohibition party ticket.

The site that Brown chose was in the southern part of what later became the state of Nebraska. It boasted rich soil, a natural stone wharf, plenty of wood, and abundant wildlife for food. Other settlers soon arrived, and the town—named for its first inhabitant—was born. In November, it became part of a new county, originally called Forney (later, Nemaha), and shortly thereafter it became the seat. During its first year, Brownville saw the opening of a general store, a school, and a sawmill. A doctor settled there, as did a lawyer, and a church was organized. Communication with the outside world was facilitated by a flatboat ferry service and Richard Brown was appointed the town's postmaster.

The town was formally laid out in 1855 by Allan L. Coate and Brownville was incorporated a year later. ". . . Several broad streets meet from different points at a Public Green, situated on a gentle elevation which commands a pretty view of the river," reported the surveyor in 1856. That year the town also got its first local paper, the

Nebraska Advertiser, which was well received even though subscription rates were quite high—$2.00 per year. A bank also commenced operations. It was a major event indeed when the firm's safe arrived by steamer.

Much of the activity in those days centered around the riverfront. Thirteen steamships plied the local waters in 1856; a year later the number rose to 47. With every steamer bringing new settlers to the area, Brownville's population rose to more than 700 by the end of 1857. ". . . From every direction comes the rattle of the carpenter's saw and hatchet, and houses spring up as by magic. . .," noted the editor of the *Advertiser*.

What did people do for recreation in such a burgeoning new community? Some enjoyed the horse races at the Newmarket Course, a track that opened outside the city. Others joined the newly formed Brownville Lyceum, Library and Literary Association, which promptly launched a series of debates. They considered, among other things, whether or not the repeal of the Missouri Compromise was right, and whether Indians had greater reason for complaint against the white man than blacks had. Some men joined the Masons or the Odd Fellows—both formed chapters in Brownville in 1857—while the women participated in sewing circles, lodge auxiliaries, and charitable societies. In 1859 the first county fair was held. The featured attractions included a two-foot carrot, a pumpkin five feet in circumference, and a white beet weighing 13 pounds.

Of course, like any other place, Brownville had its problems. On a summer night in 1857 all of the members of one family were found murdered in their beds with their house burned down around them. Claim-jumpers were not uncommon, and horse theft was so pervasive that the townsfolk had to form a protective association to stop it. As the westward migration accelerated in the years before the Civil War—spurred in part by the discovery of gold in Colorado—hundreds of wagon trains formed along the Missouri River, and many of them drew upon Brownville for supplies. Freighters, sometimes supporting as many as 60 Conestoga wagons, also stocked up here. The clothing, food, and tools they purchased were badly needed by the burgeoning new communities further west.

(Above) Now the Brownville Museum, this seven-gabled structure in the Gothic Revival style was the home of a Civil War captain named Bailey. Originally built on a site closer to the Missouri River, it was taken apart and reassembled at its present location in 1877.

(Left) Local legend has it that the Captain Bailey House on Main Street is haunted. Both Mrs. Bailey and her husband died there under questionable circumstances, and some folks maintain that both were poisoned by a widow who wanted to marry the Civil War veteran.

In 1860, the city was enjoying unprecedented prosperity. But the highlight of the year came on August 28, when the telegraph line reached town from St. Joseph, Missouri. The occasion sparked an enormous celebration with fireworks, music, and speeches.

The Nebraska Territory, clearly a land of free-soilers, was spared the anguish that tore neighboring Kansas apart in 1857/58. But, when the Civil War erupted, those in Brownville organized their own unit, Company C of the First Nebraska Volunteer Infantry. In time, they participated in the battle at Ft. Donelson in Tennessee, which introduced the nation to Ulysses S. Grant and marked the beginning of the end of the Confederacy's control over the Mississippi River valley.

(Below)From the mid-1850s to the 1880s, Brownville was a bustling, growth-oriented community, but by the time this photo was taken early in the 20th century it had become a small prairie town. The color photo below shows how the same Main Street strip looks in the 1990s.

Brownville men also saw action against the Indians. In 1863, Robert Furnas, the editor-publisher of the *Nebraska Advertiser* (and later state governor), formed a Nemaha County cavalry company, which helped rout the Sioux at the Battle of White Stone Hills in June.

During the war years, Brownville distinguished itself in one other way. Its land office became a site where settlers could register claims under the Homestead Act, passed by Congress in 1862. The town was bustling on December 31 of that year, as claimants gathered to file their chosen parcels of land the following day. Among them was Daniel Freeman, a soldier in the Union army. But Freeman had a problem. He had to rejoin his regiment in St. Louis on January 2 and couldn't wait for the business day to begin. To accommodate the young man, the office registered his claim at midnight. Thus, Brownville had the honor of processing the first land grant in the United States under the Homestead Act.

Although the community felt the war's effects, as did communities everywhere, the town continued to grow. By 1865, it was "a flourishing city of 5,000 souls," according to the *Advertiser*. A board of trade had even been formed to foster commerce. Two years later Nebraska became the 37th state in the Union.

Brownville entered the postwar years with high hopes. All that it needed to become a major city, felt the locals, was a railroad. And that was no problem. Geographically, economically, and politically, the town seemed ideally suited to serve as a railroad link between the East and the West. Finally in December 1871, after numerous, agonizing delays, 10 miles of track were laid. But the following November the ties and rails were torn up and "loaned" to a trunk line between St. Louis and Nebraska, this effort having been deemed essential to the success of the local endeavor. Worse, government land which was needed for the line was

never authorized by Congress. Finally, in 1874, the town commissioners reluctantly conceded that the dream was dead, the railroad would never be finished.

With the collapse of the railroad enterprise, Brownville's days of glory came to an end. Two years later, the county seat relocated and people left town in droves. Eventually, the population dipped as low as 174. When Willa Cather, not yet famous as a novelist, visited in 1894, she saw a place in what she called "a gentle, sunny, picturesque sort of decay, as if the old town had lain down to sleep in the hills like Rip Van Winkle."

But, like the legendary old Dutchman, Brownville woke up. Interest in its colorful past and rich architectural heritage began in the 1950s, at the behest of Nebraska-born artist Terence Dunn. Since then an active historical society has been formed, numerous craft shops, antique stores, and art galleries have opened, and dozens of old houses have been restored by private citizens. Other noteworthy residences are owned by the historical society and maintained as museums. The climax of this activity came in 1970, when Brownville was entered in the National Register of Historic Places with 32 sites. As a local historian put it, "The Phoenix has risen."

(*Opposite*) Known as the Carson House, this handsome Victorian mansion was originally the home of Richard Brown, the founder of Brownville. He sold it in 1864 to John L. Carson, a banker, who eventually built two additions to the four-room structure.

(*Right*) During its heyday Brownville enjoyed a lively river trade, with 47 steamships plying the local waters in 1857 alone. But the town's failure to attract a railroad line in the years following the Civil War brought an end to the community's leading role in commerce.

(*Above*) The paddlewheel of the *Captain Meriwether Lewis* recalls the days when Brownville's wharf bustled with activity. No fewer than 47 steamers plied the waters of the Missouri River town in the late 1850s. In 1857, 300 tons of freight were unloaded in one week alone.

(*Left*) Pictured here are the captain's quarters of the 1932 steamboat, the *Captain Meriwether Lewis*, named for the co-leader of the famous 1804 expedition. Permanently docked on the banks of the Brownville State Recreation Park, it houses the Museum of Missouri River History.

The West

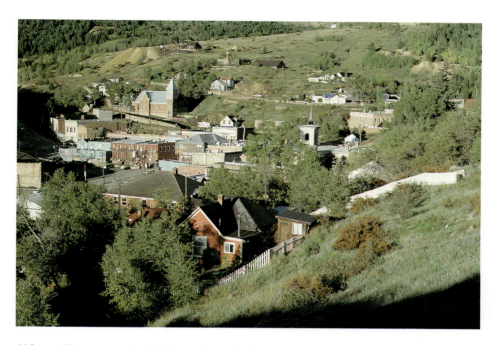

(Above) Known as the "Richest Square Mile on Earth," the area around Central City has produced more than $125 million in precious metals. The town, Colorado's first major boom city, is at an elevation of 8,500 feet, which places it more than 3,000 feet above Denver.

(Opposite) Pictured here is the famous "Face on the Bar Room Floor" in the watering hole of the Teller House hotel. It inspired the 1887 poem attributed to H. Antoine D'Arcy, in which a vagabond artist drew the countenance of his lost love Madeline on the floor and then died.

(Previous pages) The Mission San Francisco de Asís at Ranchos de Taos, Taos, New Mexico.

The rumors started flying in 1858. There was gold in Colorado! Pretty soon fortune hunters were combing the Rocky Mountains looking for precious metals.

One of those who heard the stories was a red-haired Georgian named John Gregory. Gregory had come west in 1857 and had drifted to a number of places, holding down a variety of jobs, including driving horse teams for the government. Deciding to try his luck at prospecting, he ventured forth from Fort Laramie, Wyoming late in the year, choosing Clear Creek Canyon in the north central portion of the state as a good bet. He found some gold. Not enough to stake a claim on, but Gregory shrewdly followed the stream bed until he finally reached a gulch rich in "color." By then it was January 1859, so he waited out the winter and then returned to the spot in April. On May 6, 1859, he discovered a rich vein on a hill above the gulch. This find and those nearby ultimately yielded more than $125 million dollars in precious metals, and the area became known as the "Richest Square Mile on Earth."

It did not take long for the news of Gregory's find to circulate. By the first of June, there were some one thousand

It was a red-haired Georgian named John Gregory who in May 1859 discovered the rich vein of gold that gave rise to Central City. He never put down roots in the town, however. He sold his claim, worked briefly as a free-lance prospector, and left the area by July.

tant church organization in the state, met in the home of a former slave woman until a house of worship was completed in 1872. It was most likely a "pattern church," that is, its design was probably selected from a variety of choices in a book, but its stonework was considered the best in Colorado at the time.

In addition to having a church group, Central City soon enjoyed some of the other trappings of civilization. In 1860, the U.S. mail service reached the mountains, borne by the Pony Express and the Overland Stage. There were also literary readings, clubs, and theaters. In 1861, an impresario by the name of Jack Langrishe even turned a motley collection of miners and dance hall girls into a troupe of polished stage performers. Based on his success in

Central City, Langrishe formed other troupes and they toured the mining communities of Colorado.

One of the town's crowning achievements came in 1872, when attorney and later U.S. senator Henry Teller built a four-story, brick hotel, which he named for himself. At the time, the Teller House was the finest lodging place between the Mississippi River and San Francisco. Six years later, the Central City Opera House opened. It was the first such structure in the state—Colorado having joined the Union in 1876, with Central City only one vote shy of beating out Denver as the capital.

Of course, like most other mining towns, Central City was more raucous than cultured, with an array of saloons, dance halls, and gambling parlors

prospectors working the gulch. A month later the population had reached a staggering 20,000. And a month after that, Gregory himself left the area, having sold his first claim for $21,000 and having worked as a free-lance prospector over the intervening months.

The first camp established by the miners became known as Mountain City. But the area became so crowded so quickly that other camps soon followed and these too gave rise to towns. Black Hawk, Nevada City, Lake Gulch, and Missouri Flats were among their poetic names. In the midst of this cluster emerged a group of log homes and canvas-covered structures. Because of their location, they became known as the "center," then the "city of the center," and then Central City. By the time it was officially incorporated in 1864, this burgeoning metropolis had swallowed up Mountain City and many of the other mining communities.

The first church in the area, St. James Methodist Church, was founded in 1859, the same year as the town. The congregation, the oldest Protes-

(Left) In the foreground of this photo is the bell tower constructed in 1875 to house the town's new $250 bell. Behind it is City Hall, built of logs in 1862 and later covered with clapboard. The oldest public building in Colorado, it serves today as the town marshal's office.

(Below) An old mill stands in silence, silhouetted against the promontories that ultimately yielded more than $125 million in precious metals. At one time there were well over 50 mills operating in the Central City area.

replete with ladies of the evening. Before Colorado became an organized territory in 1861, each mining district was governed by its own rules. Trials were often held in the open air and punishment for the guilty could be swift and deadly. The town's sheriff was a man by the name of Billy Cozens, who by all accounts was a fair, hard-working law enforcement officer. He was so dedicated, in fact, that on his wedding night he kept two prisoners chained to the posts of his bed. With the town jail under construction, he had no other place to keep them.

Fire—the plague of every burgeoning western town—left Central City unscathed for more than a decade. That near miraculous stroke of luck came to an end in 1874, when the city was virtually gutted by flames. But out of the ashes came a town rebuilt with fire safety in mind. The streets were laid out in a straighter fashion, buildings were constructed of bricks and stone, an adequate water supply system was established, and several volunteer fire companies were formed. As a consequence, Central City has not experienced another major fire in more than 115 years.

There is a pattern to the activities of most mining towns and Central City was no exception. Typically claims are first worked by individual prospectors using picks, pans, and sluice boxes to find ore close to the surface. These relatively primitive methods—called placer mining—then give way to shaft mining, which is both labor and capital intensive. When shaft mining commences, the lone prospector is replaced by the mine owner, the mine manager, and the banker. In Central City, the transition occurred near the end of the 1860s. Soon mine operations per se where joined by mills and smelters, where the crude ore was crushed and refined. These efforts somewhat reduced the high cost of carting ore to the transportation centers, but carrying even the refined metals down the mountains by wagon was an expensive proposition.

The Thomas House, built in 1874, was home to one family, the Thomases, for more than a century. Now a house museum operated by the Gilpin County Historical Society, this treasure-trove features furniture, paintings, jewelry, articles of clothing, and many other items of Victoriana, all original to the house.

Finally, in 1878, the Colorado Central railroad reached town. Then the mine owners only had to worry about getting their cargo from the refineries to the depot. Their solution was a unique, two-foot-narrow-gauge railroad that served the mines and mills directly. Construction on this enterprise began in May 1887 and by August of the following year more than 15 miles of track had been laid. By 1910, the Gilpin Gold Tram (Gilpin being the name of the county in which Central City is located) covered 26.46 miles and was a roaring success, serving 23 mills and 59 mines at its zenith. In March 1898, one run alone consisted of 36 cars carrying a hefty 288 tons of ore.

During its heyday, Central City attracted a number of noteworthy individuals. Perhaps the most important was Ulysses S. Grant, who came to town in 1873. To celebrate his arrival, the city fathers lined the entrance to the Teller Hotel with silver bricks—gold being considered too common—so that the president could walk on nothing but precious metal as he alighted from his coach.

Among the town's other notables was George Pullman, who got his start

(Opposite) **This row of handsome buildings lining Lawrence Street typifies the Victorian architecture of the 1870s. Central City was nearly destroyed by fire in 1874. When the town was rebuilt, brick and stone structures replaced the wooden buildings that had burned.**

in Central City as a miner and moneylender. It is said that his inspiration for the celebrated railroad sleeping car came from the bunkhouses that proliferated in Colorado's mining camps. Another moneymaking enterprise was born in the nearby hills when hatmaker John Stetson, camping in the mountains for his health, improvised on a bet a wide-brimmed hat from rabbit fur. He sold the makeshift chapeau to a Central City horseman, but when he returned to his home in Philadelphia he began to mass produce the fanciful creation. Within a year, he had to build a new factory to keep up with the demand.

Unfortunately Central City's glory days did not last as long as the Stetson hat. The productivity of the mining town had come to an end by the second decade of the 20th century. Even the Gilpin Gold Tram ceased opera-

(Top) **When the Central City Opera House was completed in 1878, it was the first structure of its kind in the state.**

(Above) **This photograph taken during the 1860s shows how Central City mining had progressed from the day of the lone prospector working with a pick, a pan, and a sluice box. The area continued to be productive until the start of the 1920s.**

(Right) **In 1932, Ann Evans and Ida Kruse McFarlane—both descended from Colorado pioneers—spearheaded an effort to restore and revitalize the Opera House. Their efforts gave birth to an opera and play festival, which continues to be an annual summer event.**

tions in January 1917. By then the town had become the setting for Tom Mix's silent movies.

Curiously, Central City's rebirth came by way of another cultural endeavor, for in 1932 the opera house was restored and the Summer Opera Festival instituted. The first production was *Camille* with Lillian Gish, and the following year Walter Houston starred in *Othello*.

Today, the Central City Opera Festival continues to draw tourists, as do the town's colorful history and rich architectural heritage. Indeed, Central City—now an easy 35-mile drive from Denver—is a Registered National Historic District with the Teller House, St. James Church, the opera house, an historical museum, several mines, and a number of restored homes open to view.

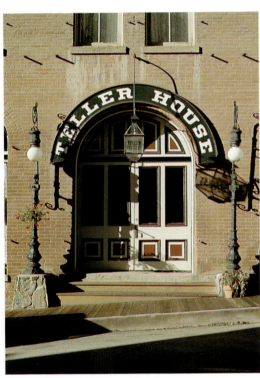

(Above) The Teller House was named for its original owner, Henry Teller, who later became one of Colorado's first two U.S. senators. When it opened in 1872, the five-story hotel was considered the finest lodging place between the Mississippi River and San Francisco. A portrait of Teller may be seen at top.

(Right) Pictured here is the main hallway of the Teller House. The statue at the foot of the stairs is Minerva. For more than a hundred years, she has supposedly brought good luck to all who rub her derrière on the way up the stairs. The tall clock in the background runs on mercury, which adjusts to barometric variations and thereby maintains the correct time. There are only two other such timepieces in the country.

188

(Above) Built in 1873, this red frame structure was originally home to Peter McFarlane, the building contractor who constructed the Central City Opera House. It is still a private residence.

(Right) The Golden Rose Inn, built in 1874, features 26 rooms, each furnished in an array of Victorian antiques and featuring a distinctive pattern of hand-screened wallpaper, made in France. The honeymoon suite is pictured here.

(Above) Around 1875 Blair Street started boasting residential structures. Then, in the 1880s, it became the town's red-light district. Most of the buildings which line the street today date from 1890 to 1910.

(Opposite) This photo taken from the cemetery offers an impressive view of the the San Juan Mountains, which were originally home to the Ute Indians and ceded to the United States by treaty in 1873. At an elevation of 9,318 feet, Silverton experienced winters so harsh that mining could only take place during the summer months.

Old Wyatt maintained that the best way to win a shootout was to take one's time, and he must have known what he was talking about because he never lost at gunplay. Still, as a shootist, Mr. Earp was not as awesome as the legends would have it. His reputation stemmed largely from one encounter, the gunfight at the O.K. Corral in Tombstone, Arizona. Two years after that frontier milestone, the former deputy marshal of Dodge City, Kansas could be found in the bustling mining town of Silverton in the San Juan mountains of southwestern Colorado. There he ran the clubrooms of a swanky saloon called the Arlington. He did not stay long, however. One day Bat Masterson and Doc Holliday arrived in town and the man the *Silverton Democrat* described as "a pleasant and affable gentleman" departed for Topeka, Kansas.

Twenty-three years before Earp came to town, the mineral wealth of the San Juan Mountains was discovered by Charles Baker, who led some 150 men into the area in 1860 and stayed for about three weeks. During the next 11 years, however, the region went unexplored, in part

(Right) The community's first house of worship, the Silverton United Church of Christ, began as the Congregational Church in August 1880. The bell tower was added 12 years later. The structure, in the Victorian Gothic style, is still in use today.

(Below) On July 13, 1882, the Denver & Rio Grande railroad reached Silverton, marking the start of a period of dramatic growth for the community. Until then, the town had been virtually inaccessible during the long winter months. The narrow-gauge railroad (operating on tracks 3 feet wide instead of the standard 4' 8½") still runs between Silverton and Durango, Colorado. A major tourist attraction, it features steam locomotives and, in some cases, coaches from the 1870s and 1880s.

because of the Civil War and in part because the San Juans were claimed by the Ute Indians.

Then in 1871 George Howard, a member of the original Baker party, and a group of prospectors entered the area. When they found gold, they used some specimens to convince William Pile, the governor of the New Mexico territory, and several other Sante Fe investors to outfit a more sophisticated survey. Because the winters were so harsh in the high elevations of the mountains, the search for precious metals was limited to the summer months.

By 1873 the camp had grown to about a hundred rugged individuals, and one mine, the Little Giant, had been established, as had a small stamp mill for processing the ore. It was in the summer of that year—after the Ute Indians had formally ceded the San Juans to the United States—that a town site was laid out. Centrally located to a group of emerging tent cities, it became known as Silverton. The name, according to a local legend, was inspired by a miner who claimed the nearby mountains bore little gold but had "silver by the ton."

By 1874 Silverton boasted a store, which also served as a site for dances, and a sawmill. Still, as one resident noted, the "buildings in the town were few and far between." Dramatic growth came quickly, however. The following year saw the opening of a drug store, a restaurant, several saloons, and a smelter. The first local newspaper, the *La Plata Miner*, premiered in July 1875, and the town's first baby—a girl—was born. Perhaps the new arrival inspired the building of a school, which also served in those early days as a church and town hall.

One of Silverton's first shootings occurred in the summer of 1875, when a drunken miner named Kelley accidently wounded another man. The town had no jail at the time, so the perpetrator was chained to the floor of a slab cabin.

An even more dramatic affair took place in 1879. It seems that on the night of August 23, two men, Harry

Cleary and someone known only as "Mexican Joe," were drinking and gambling in one of the town's saloons. When Cleary started arguing with some of the other customers, James M. Brown a part-owner of the establishment, attempted to escort him outside. There Cleary pulled a gun, shot the saloonkeeper, and ran off. The wounded man fired repeatedly at the retreating figure but to no avail. During the fracas, Hiram Ward, a one-armed night watchman, happened by and intercepted one of Brown's stray bullets. He returned fire and moments later the saloonkeeper was dead.

The man who started it all, Harry Cleary, was arrested, broken out of jail by a party of vigilantes, and hung. However, it is likely that *his* shot gave Brown no more than a flesh wound. It

A Silverton resident noted in 1874 that the "buildings in the town were few and far between." Dramatic growth came quickly, however, particularly after the railroad reached the community in 1882.

(*Above*) Silverton's main thoroughfare, Greene Street, is named for George Greene, one of the founders of the town. He was not only Silverton's first merchant, he also owned a sawmill and a smelter. Although Silverton did not initially have a central business district, one had developed on Greene Street by 1877.

193

was the night watchman, Ward, who was probably the killer. He certainly had a motive, for Brown, a member of the town council, had been trying to get him fired because of his handicap.

Despite these incidents, Silverton was not nearly as rowdy and dangerous as many other western mining towns. Much of the credit for its law-abiding ways went to the marshal, James Cart, who received a unanimous vote from the townsfolk in one election.

In 1876, Silverton was incorporated and became the seat of San Juan County. By that point, it had grown to a town of about 350 people and some hundred houses. There were two sawmills and four stores, plus the usual array of gambling parlors, saloons, hotels, and boardinghouses. Four years later, in 1880, the cornerstone was laid for the Congregational Church and the town's first major brick structure, the Posey & Wingate Building, was dedicated.

Progress was clearly being made, but in some ways Silverton remained quite primitive. For instance, the best the town could do for fire protection was a series of ditches between the buildings and the dirt streets. Indeed the risk of conflagration was so great that the town fathers made arson a hanging offense. Moreover, Silverton remained relatively isolated. At an elevation of more than 9,000 feet, it could only be reached by pack trains and, later, on primitive wagon trails, and these routes could only be traversed during the warm weather months. The local winters were so forbidding, in fact, that the mines became almost inaccessible, and many of the merchants closed their shops between November and May.

(Top) It was an 1871 party of prospectors led by George Howard, pictured here, who found the gold in the San Juan mountains. Howard had been a member of the Baker group that had first explored the region in 1860.

(Above) Today this highly ornamented building on Blair Street is a restaurant, but it began as a bordello. At the time the thoroughfare, named for one of Silverton's original founders, Thomas Blair, was rife with gambling parlors and houses of prostitution. Indeed it was the place to go in Silverton for those with a taste for the tawdrier side of life.

It was a party of prospectors in 1860 who initially discovered the riches of Colorado's San Juan Mountains, but it took 13 years for the town of Silverton to emerge as the principal community of the mining area. According to local legend, the name was inspired by a miner who claimed the mountains bore little gold but had "silver by the ton."

(Above) Built around 1886, this house in the Second Empire style, with Victorian elements in the trim, belonged to William D. Harris, a miner, and his wife, Emma, known locally as "the Russian Princess," because she was born in Odessa. Today the house, which is a bed-and-breakfast, bears the name of its second owner, John W. Wingate, a businessman who purchased it in 1890.

In 1883, two years after the gunfight at the O.K. Corral in Tombstone, Arizona, legendary lawman Wyatt Earp spent a brief period of time in Silverton, tending the clubrooms of a swanky saloon called the Arlington.

When the mail got through, it was borne by a carrier on snowshoes.

The situation changed dramatically on July 13, 1882, when the Denver & Rio Grande railroad reached town. The regular influx of goods and people made Silverton a viable community year-round. It also made profitable the production of lower-grade ores which had been too expensive to mine when freight costs were prohibitive.

Thanks in large part to the arrival of the railroad Silverton saw dramatic growth in the early 1880s, including the opening of several clothing stores,

a hardware store, and the deluxe saloon and gambling hall named the Arlington, the place that employed Wyatt Earp. There was even a restaurant whose bill of fare included duck, quail, rabbit, and oysters. For those with a taste for the tawdrier side of life there was Blair Street, where prostitution and gambling were rampant. Professional prize fights were popular. And, in 1884, the town got its own brass band. The musicianship must have left something to be desired, however, for the *Miner* urged its readers to "Boycott it! Drown it! Put it in a snowslide!"

Despite Silverton's stiff law against arson, fires could not be avoided entirely. The city's worst conflagration hit on January 10, 1890, when 10 buildings were destroyed and the damages reached an estimated $20,000. That was a mild disaster, however, for a western mining town. Later in the year, life in Silverton took a turn for the better—electric lights were introduced.

(Right) The present San Juan County Court-house was completed in 1907. By then Silverton was enjoying the peak of its mining boom, which inspired the construction of many of the town's finest public and commercial structures.

(Below) The Old Chicago Saloon on Greene Street was built in 1896 by John V. Lorenson, a photographer as well as a saloon operator, and his partner, Joe Grivetto. It was considered more respectable than the establishments on Blair Street. Today the building houses a gift shop.

(Above) Although Silverton certainly had its share of notorious characters, the town was not nearly as rowdy and dangerous as many other western mining towns. But in the early years of the 20th century, when a fellow broke the law, he could enjoy the comforts of the town jail, located behind the courthouse.

Around the turn of the century the mining boom reached its zenith, the county's population climbed to about 4,500, and many of Silverton's finest public and commercial structures—including the county courthouse, the town hall, the jail, and the Catholic church—were built. For decades thereafter, the production of zinc, lead, and precious metals continued to fuel the local economy. Although the yield declined in the 1950s, Silverton continued to be a productive mining community until the Sunnyside Mine closed in 1991.

At present, Silverton has a population of approximately 400 in winter and 700 in summer and is a treasure-trove for those with a love of the Old West. The entire town is a National Historic Landmark, with some 400 structures built between 1874 and the first decade of the 20th century. A walking tour may be found in the Silverton–San Juan Vacation Guide, available at many locations in town.

(Above) The main thoroughfare in Helena, Montana is poetically called Last Chance Gulch, the name given the site by four prospectors who saw in the area their final hope of discovering gold. The statue of a bull-wacker at right stands in a pedestrian mall.

(Opposite) The Masonic Temple at 104 Broadway was built in 1885. The third such temple in the town's history, it served the local members of the fraternal order from 1886 to 1942.

I f ever a town were founded on luck it was Helena, Montana. The good fortune belonged to four down-at-the-heels prospectors— Reginald Stanley, John Crabb, John Cowan, and J. D. Miller—known in Montana lore as the Four Georgians, even though Stanley hailed from England and Crabb and Miller were from Iowa and Alabama respectively.

Each of the "Georgians" had come to Montana to seek his fortune, but in 1864, there were no claims left to stake in the newest diggings at Alder Gulch. The word of a new discovery on the Kootenai River, nearly 400 miles away, sent them scurrying. Perhaps it never occurred to them that the rumor might have been initiated by those who wanted to depopulate the overcrowded mine fields.

On the journey, Crabb and Stanley, who were partners by then, encountered a party of miners returning from the Kootenai and learned to their dismay that no new strike awaited them. Rather than return to Alder Gulch, they teamed up with two other frustrated fortune-seekers, John Cowan and J. D. Miller, and the foursome followed the Blackfoot River into the wilderness, reaching what became known as the Prickly Pear Valley by the beginning of June

(Above) One of the Four "Georgians" who founded Helena was an Englishman named Reginald Stanley. Digging alone along the place they called Last Chance Gulch, he discovered the "color" that started the strike.

(Right) On view in the Sanders house, now a bed-and-breakfast inn, are many of the original furnishings of Col. Wilber F. Sanders, an eloquent attorney and one of Montana's first U.S. senators. The mansion was completed in 1887.

The Old Fire Tower, built on a hilltop overlooking downtown Helena, helped protect the town against the constant threat of conflagration. Helena saw nine fires during its early years. The worst—in 1874, the year that the Old Fire Tower was built—destroyed much of the business district.

1864. There they found a welcome refuge from the cold spring rains and low-lying fog. They did a bit of prospecting and then continued on their journey. By mid-July, however, they still had no found no color—as the old hands called gold. Worse, their supplies were running low and their thoughts were increasingly turning toward the approach of winter. Feeling discouraged and somewhat desperate, they decided to return to the pleasant valley on Prickly Pear Creek. By then, it represented their final hope of finding mineral wealth. They even named the ravine where they prospected Last Chance Gulch.

It was Stanley, digging by himself, who found four nuggets on the gulch's bedrock. He called to his partners and the four dug through the night. The next day when they returned to their camp, they knew their last chance had paid off.

Mining law prevented them from simply hoarding the discovery for themselves. They had to announce it. But, wise in the ways of the trade, they carefully chose their own claims and established laws for the camp first. Then, two of the partners returned to Alder Gulch to obtain supplies and to reveal their find.

It didn't take long for the new site to take on the trappings of a typical bustling mining camp. "The streets were crowded with gaily shirted miners," one of the "Georgians," Reginald

Stanley, later recalled. "Mexicans with bands of broncos careened through the main business thoroughfares. The shouting oratory of auctioneers was heard above the din of tramping horses and the noisy explosions of bibulous throngs day and night." At a meeting in October 1864, 200 denizens of the camp voted to change the name from Last Chance to Helena—pronounced He-LEEN-a. The suggestion came from one John Summerville, who sought to honor a town by that name in Scott County, Minnesota.

In addition to rowdy miners, gamblers, and ladies of the night, the new discovery brought the trappings of civilization. By the end of 1865, the community boasted a day school, its first religious edifice, the Methodist Episcopal Church, and its own newspaper, the *Radiator*. In 1867 there were 188 commercial establishments and six banks. By 1870, when the U.S. census was taken, Helena had a population of 3,106 and was the largest city in the Montana territory.

Among those who made their fortunes here were Tom Cruse, an Irishman who came to the territory in 1866 and found his bonanza, the Drum Lumman strike, 10 years later. In 1884, he sold his claim to an English syndicate for more than one million dollars and thereafter devoted much of his time to philanthropic endeavors, including the building of the state capitol and the Cathedral of St. Helena. A Kentuckian, Samuel T. Hauser, started as a miner and then got into banking in 1865. By the time he died in 1914, his empire embraced railroading, cattle ranching, commerce, and freighting, and no one in the state had greater political influence. Wilbur Fisk Sanders, an attorney who hailed from

New York State and Ohio, prosecuted the case against the notorious Henry Plummer in Virginia City (Plummer, the town sheriff, had used his position to support a secret life of robbery and murder). An ardent Republican, Sanders became one of Montana's first two senators after statehood. His mansion at 328 N. Ewing Street still stands as a bed-and-breakfast inn and many of his original furnishings are still on view. As for the Four Georgians, they had as many as 70 men on their payroll in 1865 and 1866. During the time they worked their claims, they netted some $170,000 in gold dust.

Despite continued growth, Helena experienced severe hardship in the 1870s. Indeed, the Panic of 1873 and a devastating fire a year later nearly brought the town to ruin. But, in 1875, the community had recovered sufficiently to supplant Virginia City as the territorial capital. Six years later, Helena was incorporated.

(Above) This stately Victorian house was the residence of Conrad Kohrs, perhaps the largest cattle baron in Montana at the turn of the century. His ranch, the Grant-Kohrs Ranch near Deer Lodge, Montana, is a national historic site, administered by the National Park Service.

(Left) This photo, taken in about 1890, shows the First National Bank building at the northeast corner of Grand and Main. As the color photo below indicates, the building has changed little over the years. Known today as the Securities Building, it now houses offices and penthouse apartments.

(Right) One of Helena's leading citizens was Kentuckian Samuel T. Hauser, who began as a miner and then got into banking. By the time he died in 1914, his empire embraced railroading, cattle ranching, commerce, and freighting, and no one in the state had greater political influence.

(Below) The mansion pictured here was originally the home of Samuel T. Hauser, who became the territorial governor of Montana in 1885. Purchased in 1969 by former governor and Mrs. Tim Babcock, it is known today by both owners' names.

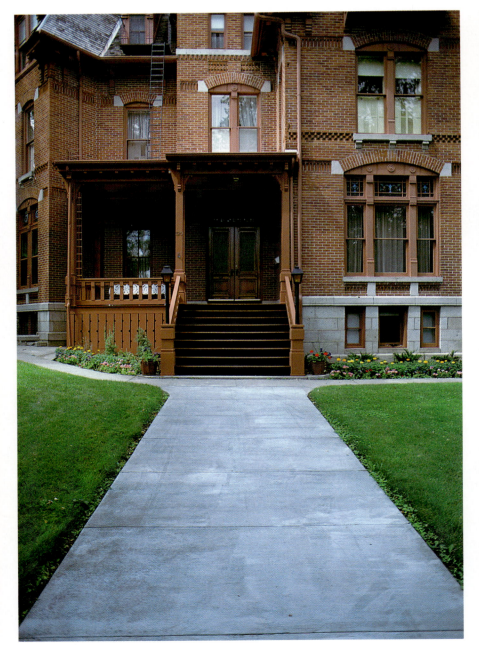

(Above) The French Renaissance rotunda of the state capitol features four circular paintings of frontier types, two of which—the prospector and the Native American—are visible in this photo. These works were part of the original decoration completed in 1902.

(Left) The Montana capitol, which was dedicated on July 4, 1902, was designed by Charles Emlen Bell and John Hackett Kent. The residents of Council Bluffs, Iowa moved to Helena after they were awarded the commission in 1898.

One might wonder why the town that had once been called Last Chance did not go the way of so many other boom-and-bust mining camps. Part of the reason lay in the town's location. Sitting as it did on the major east-west and north-south wagon trails, it became a focal point for trade and shipping. Large mining companies, which replaced individual prospectors when the placer mines gave out, headquartered there. The fertile Prickly Pear Valley could support farming and ranching. And, finally, a group of farsighted businessmen formed a board of trade in 1877 to insure the town's future. "Had it not been for the grim determination and uncompromising attitude, even selfishness of Helena's old timers," wrote local historian William C. Campell in *From the Quarries of Last Chance Gulch*, "it is probable that cattle would be grazing on Main Street today, and this city would be a 'ghost' similar to Bannack." The board of trade's crowning achievement came in 1882, when a line on the Northern Pacific railroad was extended to Helena, bringing a real boost to the local economy, with as many as 22 trains pulling in and out of town every day. At this point—and for no reason that anyone today can discern—He-LEEN-a became known as HEL-en-a.

The 1880s were the highwater mark for what was then called the Queen City of the Rockies. Local entrepreneurs erected imposing mansions, and impressive stone and brick commercial structures—called blocks—came to dominate what had once been Last Chance Gulch (and was by then Main Street). Significant examples of the Gothic Revival, French Second Empire, and Romanesque styles of architecture abounded and electricity, telephones, and trolley cars became commonplace. The population in 1890 stood at nearly 14,000.

Thus, when it came time to select the state capital—Montana having achieved statehood in 1889—Helena was the logical choice. But Anaconda had the support of copper baron Mar-

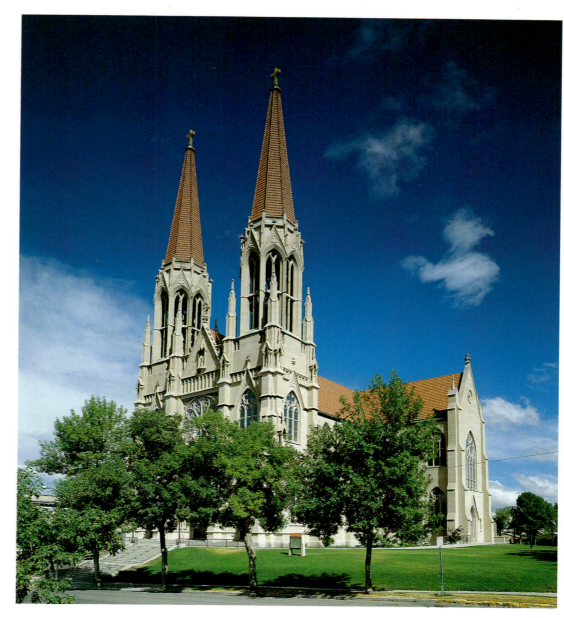

cus Daly. Finally, in 1894, with the backing of Daly's arch rival, William A. Clark, the Queen City of the Rockies triumphed over her upstart competition and five years later the cornerstone was laid for the new capitol building. Designed by architects Charles Emelen Bell and John Hacket Kent for less than $500,000, the Neo-classical structure featured exterior walls of sandstone quarried near Columbus, Montana, and a dome of copper sheeting, atop which stood the figure of *Miss Liberty*.

Helena may have won the battle to become the state's capital, but the town's golden years ended with the Depression of 1893. Since then the once sprightly mining and commercial center has become a more sedate place. Still, it weathered record cold in the winter of 1927, one of the worst fires in its history in 1928, and an earthquake in 1935 that caused $2.5 million in

The Cathedral of St. Helena was designed by O. A. Von Herbulis of Washington, D.C, who modeled it after a cathedral in Cologne, Germany. Featuring stained glass windows made in Bavaria, this sweeping Gothic building was begun in 1908 and completed 16 years later.

property damages. The state and federal government are the city's number one and number two employers and the population is largely white collar. Indeed, 26 percent of the residents over the age of 25 years are college educated (the national average is 16 percent). An urban renewal program in the 1960s and 1970s saw the destruction of a number of Helena's old commercial buildings. Nonetheless, the downtown area today features nearly a hundred historic structures, of which 53 are itemized in a brochure sponsored by the City of Helena and the Helena Downtown Business Improvement District.

(Above) Pictured here is one of the community's many antique and art dealers. The shop is located in the farming village of Ránchos de Taos, founded by Spanish settlers in 1617.

(Opposite) This window in the home of Mabel Dodge Luhan was painted by the celebrated novelist, D. H. Lawrence, who lived there for several six-month periods between 1922 and 1925. Mrs. Luhan was an heiress and patron of the arts who married an Indian, Antonio Luhan, after divorcing her third husband.

"God's in charge of everything that happens at Taos!" declared a locally prominent physician at the turn of the century. Looking at the quaint town today, one might well applaud the Almighty's handiwork.

The community's history is long, dating back to the Anasazi Indians, who first came to the valley of the Sangre de Cristo mountains around 900 A. D. They were pit house dwellers who farmed and hunted for their sustenance. In time, raiding nomadic tribes led them to band together in pueblos. One of these, Taos pueblo, whose name is thought to be derived from an Indian word meaning "Red Willow," was built around 1350 A. D. Well-situated on the trails of a number of tribes to the north, south, and west, Taos pueblo became a principal trading center and later the site of formal trade fairs at which such valuables as buffalo hides, dried meat, corn, and squash were bartered. Spaniards first appeared in the region in 1540, when members of Francisco Vasquez de Coronado's expedition came looking for gold. Failing to find the fabled Seven Cities of Cibola, they pressed on. Fifty-eight years later, however, Spanish settlers came to stay. Their leader was Don Juan de Oñate, the son

(*Opposite*) Built in the late 18th century, the Mission San Francisco de Asís at Ranchos de Taos is well known from paintings by Georgia O'Keeffe and photographs by Paul Strand and Ansel Adams. Their images, like the photo shown here, tend to emphasize the structure's thick adobe walls and massive buttresses.

(*Left*) Two miles north of town stands Taos Pueblo, more properly known as San Gerónimo de Taos. Built around 1300 A. D., this World Heritage Site is composed of two multistory dwellings separated by a stream. The pueblo is presently home to about 1,200 people.

of a silver baron who had arrived in the New World as a soldier when he was in his teens. Perhaps it was grief over the death of his wife, who passed away prematurely in the late 1580s, that led Oñate to turn his attention north, but in any event the 46-year-old veteran of numerous Indian campaigns departed New Spain in 1598 with a force of 500, ready to claim what became New Mexico for himself and his king.

In extending Spanish authority over the Indians, Oñate was not above using brute force. When one pueblo offered resistance, for example, he ordered that a foot be amputated from every male villager over the age of 25. Still, in accordance with the dictates of King Philip III, he also allowed each indigenous community to keep 17,000 acres of land (one square league) for itself, a beneficence that some might question since, before Oñate's arrival, the Indians had owned *everything*. Nevertheless

(Above) The Sante Fe Trail, seen here in an artist's rendering, extended from Missouri to New Mexico. Pioneered by William Bucknell in 1821, it led thereafter to an influx of Anglos into the territory.

(Left) Trader Charles Bent became the first governor of the territory after it was annexed by the United States in 1846, but he was killed shortly thereafter when the citizens of Taos revolted against the Yankee invaders.

(Top) Home to one of the town's leading merchants was the Martinez Hacienda, built with massive adobe walls in 1780. The residence, which grew to include 21 rooms, was structured around two courtyards. There are no exterior windows, the better to protect the occupants from Indian raids.

(Above) The Martinez Hacienda is named for Don Antonio Severino Martinez, who acquired the structure when it consisted of only four rooms. Today the hacienda reflects the lifestyle of a large and prominent family during the Spanish colonial period.

(Right) Located in the heart of town, the Taos Inn is listed on the National Register of Historic Places. Shown here is the picturesque lobby whose Moorish style fountain rises from the place where the town well originally stood.

it was a concession that the British never extended to the indigenous peoples of their colonies.

Oñate reached Taos in July 1598 and named Francisco Zamora as pastor of the local mission two months later. For the Spanish the opportunity to convert Native Americans to the Catholic religion was a paramount reason for colonization, second only to the quest for gold, and Zamora went about his mission with customary zeal.

Oñate, who had hoped to find riches in New Mexico, was disappointed with the colony. Ironically, the gold and silver that he sought was there for the taking, but he, like those who came before him, failed to find them. King Philip was also unhappy with the New Mexican adventure. In 1607, he fired Oñate as provincial governor and even toyed with the idea of abandoning the colony entirely. What stopped him was an enthusiastic report from the Franciscans, who claimed 8,000 converts in New Mexico.

The Spanish village of Ranchos de Taos was settled in 1615, a few miles from the pueblo. The first colonists were attracted by the valley's abundance of water and timber, but rela-

tions with the indigenous people were difficult, at best. Finally, in 1680, the Indians rose up against the colonists under the leadership of a medicine man named Po-pe. It was an extremely well-coordinated campaign, the most successful Native American uprising in history, and when it ended all of the white settlers and priests in New Mexico had either been killed or driven out. It took until 1692 for the Spanish to return to reconquer the province. Taos Pueblo fell in 1694, revolted again two years later, and was reconquered once more.

In the years that followed, Spanish Taos remained primarily an agrarian community with most colonists living on farms or small ranches. During the 18th century, crop production was enhanced by a series of irrigation ditches known as *acequias*, which brought badly needed water from the mountains to the arid southwestern land. Trade in these years was restricted by Spanish authority to the mother country and to other Spanish colonies, namely Mexico. A caravan typically made the six-month journey to Taos along the Camino Real (the King's Road) every three or four years. In time, commerce between Taos and Chihuahua, a new city in central Mexico, accelerated, with pack trains going south annually after each fall's trade fair, bearing wool, sheep, candles, buffalo skins, and wheat. Those coming back carried linens, silver, ironwork, chocolate, and tools.

One of the community's leading merchants was Don Antonio Severino Martinez, who arrived in Taos with his family in 1804. His youngest son, Juan Pascual, carried on the family business after his death in 1827 while Don Antonio's eldest son, Antonio Jose, served as the priest of Taos parish. Padre Martinez also opened a school in 1826, whose textbooks he published himself on his own printing press, the first such device west of the Mississippi River. In addition, he published a weekly newspaper—the first in the

For 25 years, Kit Carson and his family lived in a single-story, 12-room adobe near the Taos plaza. The kitchen of the famed scout's home is pictured here.

area—and, along with his brother, served in the territorial legislature.

American mountain men started appearing in Taos as early as 1750 and their numbers increased with the Louisiana Purchase of 1803. More Anglos began arriving in the 1820s, after Mexico won independence from Spain and control over New Mexico passed to the Mexican government, which opened up the borders between its lands and those of the United States. The westward journey eased dramatically in 1821, when William Bucknell pioneered the Sante Fe Trail, which extended from Missouri to New Mexico.

As had the Indians and Spanish before them, the Americans found Taos to be an excellent trading center. Among those who set up shop here were Charles Bent and Ceran St. Vrain, who had previously owned a highly successful trading post in Colorado. But the most famous newcomer was Christopher Carson. Born in Kentucky in 1809, Kit, as he was known, first came to New Mexico at the age of 16 with a wagon train led by Charles

(Right) The Kentucky-born Christopher "Kit" Carson came to New Mexico at the age of 16. Thereafter he gained renown as a fur trapper and mountain man, winning his greatest fame as guide for the expeditions of Charles Frémont in 1842 and 1843/44.

Bent. Thereafter he gained renown as a fur trapper and mountain man, winning his greatest fame as guide for the expeditions of Charles Frémont in 1842 and 1843/44. In 1842 his wife, an Arapaho woman, died, and a year later he married Josepha Jaramillo, a member of one of Taos' oldest families. As a wedding present, he purchased and modified a single-story, 12-room adobe near the Taos plaza and lived there with his wife and children for 25 years, although his adventures frequently took him far from home.

In 1846 war broke out between the United States and Mexico, and an expeditionary force of 2,700 men under the command of Gen. Stephen Kearny was dispatched from Ft. Levenworth, Kansas, to secure New Mexico for the Americans. Santa Fe fell without resistance, but on January 19, 1847, after Kearny had departed for California, the denizens of Taos revolted against the Yankee invaders, murdering, among others, Charles Bent, who had recently become the first U.S. governor of the territory. Dispatched to Taos at the head of a retaliatory force, Col. Sterling Price ended the affair with an assault on the Taos Pueblo church that left some 150 insurrectionists dead and the church in ruins.

Little changed in Taos between the end of the Mexican War and the outbreak of the Civil War in 1861. During the nation's bloodiest conflict, the community remained loyal to the Union, with local volunteers helping

(Above) The town plaza remains the focus point of Taos life. The La Fonda Hotel, which can be seen in the background of this photo, stands on the site that was once occupied by the Bent–St. Vrain store.

(Right) This photo taken around 1880 shows a couple of itinerant merchants in Taos Plaza. No doubt these dashing gents furthered the town's long history as a commercial center, a history extending back to the days before the Spanish conquistadors when major trade festivals were attended by the Commanche, the Apache, the Navajo, and other nomadic tribes.

to fill the ranks of a New Mexico regiment commanded by Kit Carson. On March 27–28, 1862, they distinguished themselves at the Battle of Glorieta Pass, a Union victory that virtually ended the Confederacy's attempt to secure the gold fields of the West.

Shortly after the war's conclusion, gold was discovered in the mountains above Taos, and mining has played a role in the local economy ever since. But the community was bypassed by the railroad, which terminated in Sante Fe instead, and as a consequence Taos has remained relatively isolated. It was its picturesque charm, as well as the beauty of the surrounding countryside, that attracted artists, such as Ernest Blumenschein and Bert Phillips, at the end of the 19th century. The art colony which they established in town became highly celebrated for its landscapes and depictions of a rapidly disappearing way of life. Over the ensuing decades, some of America's most celebrated photographers and painters, notably Georgia O'Keeffe, Ansel Adams, and Paul Strand, have furthered the tradition.

Today Taos' connection with the arts continues with some 80 local galleries. The homes of several celebrated citizens—Kit Carson, Don Antonio Severino Martinez, and Ernest Blumenschein—have been restored and are open to public view. And the crowning glory of the area, indeed one of the most important historic structures in America—Taos Pueblo, about two miles outside of town—remains largely as it has always been, presently housing about 1,200 residents.

(Above) Parts of the home of Ernest L. Blumenschein date from 1790, but much of the structure was built at the artist's behest after he and his wife purchased the property in 1919. Blumenschein, seen at left in his studio in 1926, was one of the founders of the celebrated art colony that flourished in Taos during the early decades of the 20th century.

(Below) The distinctive Fechin House was the home of Russian-born artist Nicolai Fechin, who arrived in Taos in 1927. Fechin designed the house himself and decorated the interior with an impressive array of wood carvings.

SALT LAKE CITY

UTAH

(Above) Downtown Salt Lake City today is distinguished by many 19th- and early-20th-century structures which are often found next to more modern buildings in an eclectic yet comfortable mixture of styles. Pictured here are the the courthouse (right), a Neo-classical structure built between 1903 and 1906, and the Boston Building (left), constructed only a few years later but reflective of the new skyscrapers then emerging in cities like New York, Chicago, and St. Louis.

(Opposite) This is the elaborate hallway of the City and County Office Building at Washington Square, built between 1891 and 1894. Modeled after the City Hall in London, it features more than a hundred rooms and initially cost more than $1 million to complete.

He was a carpenter by trade, living in Mendon, New York in the late 1820s with his wife and two children. He probably would not have believed it if someone had told him that in less than 20 years he would be the head of an entire church, leading his followers across a vast land in search of a place where they could worship in peace. But in 1844 that is exactly what Brigham Young had become and exactly what he was about to do. In keeping with such daring, he had no idea in setting out where he and his people would end up. He was sure, however, that he would recognize the right place when he saw it.

The religion that Brigham Young came to head, the Church of Jesus Christ of Latter-day Saints, was founded in 1830 by Joseph Smith, a young farmhand from upper New York State. Almost from the beginning the Mormons—as they came to be known—were harassed by other segments of the community, in part for their exclusiveness and in part for their religious beliefs which, among other things, proclaimed Smith (and later Young) to be God's prophet and which came in time to embrace plural marriages.

(Below) The Church of Jesus Christ of Latter-day Saints was founded in 1830 by Joseph Smith, a young farmhand from upper New York State. In 1844, he was murdered by a mob of irate citizens in Nauvoo, Illinois, the community to which the Mormons had fled.

(Below) The home and official residence of Brigham Young was this two-story adobe structure built in 1854. Boasting six columns on the facade, it was named the Beehive House, for the wooden beehive—a Mormon symbol of industriousness—above the front cupola.

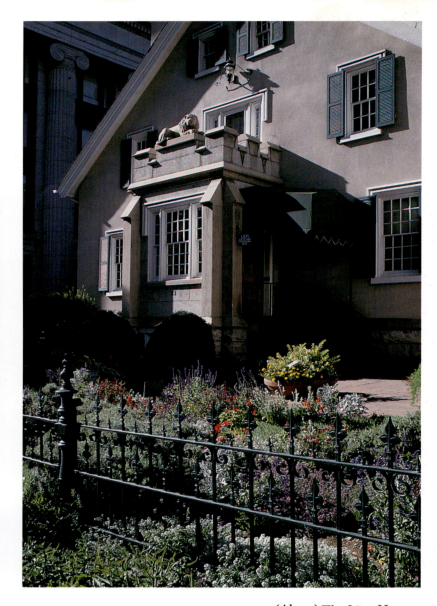

(Above) The Lion House at 63 East South Temple was built in 1856 to house some of Brigham Young's wives and children. Designed by Truman O. Angell, the architect of the Salt Lake Temple, the house gets its name from the stone lion crouched over the first-floor portico, which is visible in this photo.

(Left) Smith's successor as head of the Mormon church was Brigham Young, a carpenter by trade. It was he who led the Saints west where they could find a place of their own.

Between 1831 and 1844 Smith and his followers fled to Kentland, Ohio, Independence, Missouri, and Nauvoo, Illinois, encountering intolerance from their neighbors in each of these locales. Finally, on June 27, 1844, Smith was murdered by a mob of irate citizens.

The religion might have dissolved thereafter but for Young. Brother Brigham, as they called him, determined that the Mormons would travel west to find a place removed from the rest of humanity where they would at last be able to live and worship as they pleased.

(Below) Pictured here is the sitting room of the Beehive House, appropriately furnished in handsome pieces from the Victorian Age. One of the designers of the home was Truman O. Angell, whose sister, Mary Ann, married Brigham Young. She was the only one of the patriarch's 27 wives to live here during his lifetime.

By 1846, Saints were encamped across the plains of Iowa, preparing for the big trek west the following year, and in April 1847, an advance group of 143 men, three women, and two children reached the Rocky Mountains. Two months later, they were headed for the north central part of what is now the state of Utah, inspired by glowing accounts of the Salt Lake Valley from trappers like Jim Bridger and Jedidiah Smith and the "Pathfinder," Capt. John C. Frémont.

"We could not refrain from a shout of joy . . . the moment this grand and lovely scenery was within our view," wrote one of the church elders, Orson Pratt. Indeed, the valley seemed well suited to the Mormons' needs. The soil was good, there was ample timber for building, and the climate was pleasant enough. There was even an abundance of water from nearby mountain

streams. Perhaps best of all the valley was isolated from other frontier communities, so at last the Saints could be free from outside harassment. Indeed the region was not even part of the United States. It was owned by Mexico and would be until the following year when the Treaty of Guadalupe Hidalgo ceded it—along with Mexico's other American lands—to the victors of the recent war between the United States and Mexico.

When Young first laid eyes on the valley on July 23, 1847, he knew the journey had come to an end. "This is the right place," he said matter-of-factly, "Drive on." Eleven days later Pratt began laying out the city and on August 7 the church leaders commenced their selection of lots.

Within the first four months, the number of residents in what became known as Great Salt Lake City reached

(Above) Located at the southwest corner of Temple Square is Assembly Hall, designed by Obed Taylor and dedicated in January 1882. This structure of rough-cut granite and glistening white spires was built at the behest of Brigham Young shortly before his death. Restored between 1979 and 1981, it is still used today for church services and community functions.

Life in Salt Lake City wasn't all work for the industrious settlers. Among other things, the town boasted an active dramatic society, some of whose members are seen here in *The Wrong Bird*. Brigham Young himself was among the thespians' supporters.

nearly 1,700, and by the first year the figure had grown to 5,000. In 1850, the city was incorporated, and its administration passed to a city council consisting of a mayor, four aldermen, and nine councillors. In that same year Utah became a U.S. territory with Brigham Young as governor and supervisor of Indian Affairs.

Young wanted Great Salt Lake City to be a mercantile and manufacturing rather than an agricultural center. Consequently only about a third of the citizens were farmers at the outset and that number declined as time went by. Nevertheless, Brother Brigham expected the town's citizens to be self-sufficient, growing most of the food they needed for themselves.

The industrious Mormons quickly set about building their new community. The first year saw the construction of a school, a gristmill, and a fort for protection against the Indians. A large field for communal crops was seeded outside the garrison. But the first season was horrible, with a late frost and an infestation of crickets destroying the crops and nearly starving out the settlers. Several irrigation ditches were also built, with each man in town participating in their construction and maintenance and each receiving water rights in return.

As the only major settlement between the Midwest and the Pacific Coast, Great Salt Lake City prospered as a trading center in the the years before the Civil War, when large numbers of settlers and gold-seekers made the trek west. To meet the demand for goods, a general store opened in 1849 and another commenced operations the following year. A post office was established in the winter of 1849 and in June 1850 the first local newspaper, the *Deseret News* premiered. And the city's biggest building project, the Salt Lake Temple, began in 1853. This imposing granite structure in the Gothic Revival style took a total of 40 years to complete.

Of course life in the growing town wasn't all work. There were concerts, lectures on a wide variety of topics, and even a dramatic society. Among the thespians' supporters was Brother Brigham himself, who reportedly said, "The people must have amusement as well as religion."

The most critical event of the 1850s was the Mormons' conflict with the federal government. From the beginning, Young's dream of a community living in splendid isolation failed to materialize, but the degree to which the State of Deseret—as the Mormons called their territory—had become part of the United States was made apparent in 1857, when President James Buchanan decided to replace the Mormon leader as governor of the territory and dispatched a force of 2,500 men under Col. Albert Sidney Johnston to insure the orderly transfer of power to the new appointee, Alfred Cumming.

Young learned of the military expedition on July 24, 1857, and without

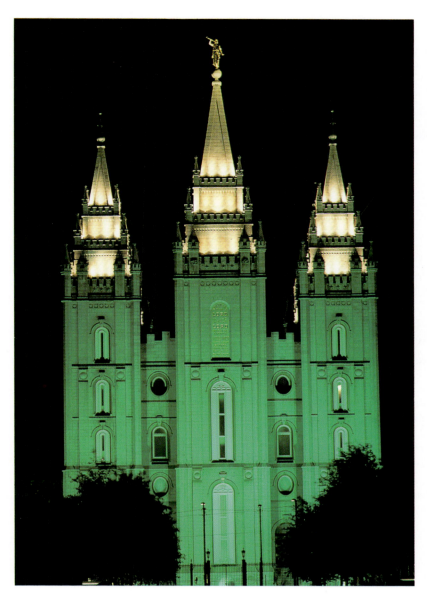

(*Left*) Dominating Temple Square is the massive Gothic Revival temple that took 40 years to complete. The grey granite structure, which soars to a height of 210 feet, was designed by Truman O. Angell, one of Brigham Young's brothers-in-law. It was dedicated in 1893.

(*Below*) The Tabernacle in Temple Square is an architectural marvel. Built in 1867, it is huge— 250 feet long and 150 feet wide, with a seating capacity of 7,000—yet it has no supporting columns. This feat was accomplished by Henry Grow, a Pennsylvania bridge builder. The structure owes much of its fame to the internationally renowned choir that sings here.

This elaborate stonework is from the Boston Building at 9 Exchange Place, originally owned by Samuel Newhouse and named for his mining company, Boston Consolidated. Its twin, the Newhouse Building, was named for the copper king himself. Both structures were designed by Henry Ives Cobb and completed in 1909.

Constructed between 1909 and 1911, the Kearns Building is evocative of the style of celebrated architect Louis Sullivan, the "father of the skyscraper." Designed by Parkinson and Bergstrom of Los Angeles, the 10-story structure was owned by Thomas Kearns, a mining entrepreneur who also served in the U.S. Senate and was part-owner of the Salt Lake Tribune.

One of most impressive residences in the city, the McCune Mansion at 200 North Main, was built for Alfred W. McCune, who made his fortune building railroads. While he initially wanted a bungalow free from ostentation, he ended up with a house that featured tiles imported from Holland, mahogany from South America, and oak from Great Britain.

hard information as to its purpose, assumed that it was an invasion. Consequently, he declared martial law, called out the militia, and began to make plans for war. He also dispatched small bands of raiders to Wyoming, where their harassment of Johnston's army forced the soldiers to halt for the winter at the remains of Fort Bridger. Meanwhile, Young, thinking better of taking on the might of the United States, made plans to flee once more with his followers to a destination unknown. The evacuation had actually commenced when Thomas L. Kane, a sympathetic non-Mormon, helped Young and the new governor reach an understanding by which Young gave up the governorship but remained head of the church, and the army agreed not to settle in Great Salt Lake City but to establish its own fort, Camp Floyd, southwest of town.

With the army nearby for protection, outsiders began prospecting the region—an activity Young had always discouraged— and their findings set off a mild mining boom in the mid-1860s. These efforts further enhanced the local economy, but they also brought to the community a greater number of gentiles—as the Mormons called outsiders—and significantly expanded the newcomers' power base. The rift between the Mormons and non-Mormons became so great that in 1865/66

the Saints instituted a boycott of the town's gentile merchants, and in 1868—the year that "Great" was dropped from the town's name and it became just Salt Lake City—they formed a church-controlled company called the Zion's Cooperative Mercantile Institution. In time, the ZCMI became the parent of a highly successful chain of stores, many of them privately owned. Finally, in 1870, the gentiles countered by forming their own political party, the Liberals, and the Mormons responded with an organization of their own, the People's party.

Despite the Saints' efforts, the influence of the gentile community could not be contained and the first non-Mormon mayor, George M. Scott, was elected in 1890. Two years later he was succeeded by Robert N. Baskin, also a gentile. This fair-minded attorney brought about a healing that resulted in the demise of the religious political parties.

Except for a brief setback during the Depression of 1893, the last decades of the 19th century were a time of tremendous growth for Salt Lake City. Although geographic considerations mandated that Ogden become the venue for the transcontinental railroad, a line connecting the two Utah cities was completed on January 10, 1870, and this kept Salt Lake City in the forefront of regional trade and commerce.

By 1880, the population had climbed to 20,800, and the business district was lined with shops and businesses of every description. There were also factories, foundries, and breweries, and a variety of establishments associated with the production of precious metals. Perhaps nothing indicated the passing of the old era more than the death of Brigham Young in 1877. He left behind 17 widows (of the 27 women he married during his lifetime).

Thereafter the development of Salt Lake City proceeded as it did in most other major urban centers, with periods of decline, such as the Great Depression, in which the city was hit harder

Built in 1915, the state capitol was designed by Utah's leading architect, Richard K. A. Kletting. At a cost of nearly $3 million, it boasts a dome 285 feet high and covered in Utah copper. Massasoit, the bronze statue out front, is by Utah sculptor Cyrus Dallin.

than most, and periods of growth, such as the years of World War II, when Salt Lake City found new life as a center for defense-related industries.

Today the city is distinguished by the continuing presence of the Church of Jesus Christ of Latter-day Saints, which not only represents the majority of the town's citizens but is a large landowner in the downtown area. The city boasts a host of distinguished 19th-century buildings which stand next to 20th-century newcomers in an eclectic but comfortable mix of architectural styles. Even amid the bustle of a modern metropolis, one can see evidence of the carefully planned, utopian community that began here 145 years ago.

In 1857 President James Buchanan dispatched a force of 2,500 men under Col. Albert Sidney Johnston (left) to replace Brigham Young as governor of the Utah territory. Thanks to the intercession of a sympathetic non-Mormon named Thomas L. Kane, bloodshed was averted between the soldiers, seen above entering Salt Lake City, and the Mormons.

(Above) At an elevation of 6,147 feet, Austin, Nevada rests about halfway up Pony Canyon in the Toiyabe Mountains. It became the hub for a network of mining camps that emerged in the Reese River Valley during the 1860s silver strike.

(Opposite) Seen here is a closeup of the brick Austin Hotel, which was built sometime prior to 1870 by George Watt. At the time, the town boasted two hostelries and three boardinghouses.

There was no doubt about it, the Reese River Navigation Company was a brilliant idea. According to its elaborate prospectus, the firm expected to make a huge profit from the new silver bonanza in central Nevada by transporting ore-laden barges down the Reese River to the railhead at Battle Mountain, thereby avoiding excessive overland shipping costs. Thousands of dollars were raised for the venture. There was only one problem. During most of the year, the river could hardly support a canoe, much less a barge heaped with silver.

The outlandish Reese River Navigation Company was just one of many dubious schemes inspired by the payload discovered in the Toiyabe Mountains' Pony Canyon during the spring of 1862. Ironically the man who found it, a Pony Express station-hand named William M. Talcott, wasn't even looking for it. He was simply out rounding up stray horses when his eye fell on an intriguing outcropping. He gathered some samples and had them assayed in Virginia City. When they proved to be rich in silver, he and several others organized the area into a mining district that they named for the Reese River.

Soon hundreds of fortune-seekers were camped out at the foot of the canyon, and their collection of tents, shacks, and dugouts had taken on the aspects of a town, which they called Clifton. As the influx continued, a new community emerged about halfway up the canyon. At the behest of a Texan among them, the town was named for Stephen F. Austin, the leader of the early American settlers in what became the Lone Star State.

Initially Clifton, which enjoyed a good location and an already thriving community, seemed to have little to fear from the new town, but Austin's founding fathers cleverly offered free business lots to merchants who would help them build a road up the Pony Canyon to their town. This thoroughfare helped Austin become the area's main stagecoach terminus and, as a consequence, it overtook Clifton in the race for local supremacy. Finally, in the fall of 1863, Austin became the capital of the newly formed Lander County (named for a Nevada Indian fighter and road builder, Frederick W. Lander) and Clifton virtually disappeared.

In the days that followed, the strike continued to attract droves of newcomers. One observer on a trip between Austin and Virginia City counted 274 freight teams, 19 passenger wagons, three pack trains, 69 horsemen, and 31 people on foot, all heading for the new diggings. An incredible 6,000 mining and milling companies were incorporated in the Reese River district during its first three years, not all of them on the up and up. Thanks to the previous success of the Comstock Lode, anything associated with Nevada drew the interest of investors back East and in Europe. Many of these fortune-seekers simply kissed their investments goodbye, but others did quite well for, during its heyday, the district yielded more than $50 million worth of precious metals.

To meet the needs of the townsfolk—whose numbers were estimated at 7,000 by the fall of 1863—Austin boasted a wide range of commercial establishments, including bakeries, barber shops and, breweries. The International Hotel, which had originally stood in Virginia City, was moved to town by wagon. There was even a branch of the YMCA, the only one in early Nevada history. A weekly newspaper, the Reese River *Reveille*, commenced publication in May 1863. It cost a hefty 50 cents a copy—the price of a *New York Times* today—but then most things in Austin were expensive. A hundred-pound sack of flour, for example, cost $20 and a cord of fire-

(*Top*) The town was named, at the behest of a Texan among the first settlers, for Stephen F. Austin, pictured here. Austin was the leader of the early American colonists in what became the Lone Star State.

(*Above*) In 1897, Stokes Castle was built atop a hill some miles from town to serve as the summer home for mine-owner Anson P. Stokes. The three-story structure featured such ammenities as balconies, fireplaces, and a sundeck, but its owner used the place only for a very brief period of time.

wood ran $15. Unlike many frontier newspapers, however, the *Reveille* was not dependent for information on publications elsewhere; Austin was on the transcontinental telegraph line.

In the early days, Austin also had one other thing that distinguished it from many other western towns—camels. These desert creatures were imported to carry heavy loads of salt to the mines. The camels did not last long, however. When a nearer source of salt was found, they passed from the local scene.

Austin was wild, like most booming mining towns. There were frequent shootings and stage robberies, but few western communities ever had a night like the one Austin experienced on July 18, 1863, when a newcomer from Illinois named William Cornell decided that everyone in town was out to kill him. On the theory that he should strike at his would-be assailants first, he grabbed an ax and proceeded to attack anyone who crossed his path. He ran through the streets, into a saloon, even into a clothing store, and when he was through, he had badly wounded at least six men, including his own partner. He was found near Clifton the next day with a gash in the back of his head and his throat cut, leading many to conclude that he had turned the ax on himself.

Although Austin was certainly raucous, it had its cultured side too. The news of the silver strike reached quite a few families en route to California and some of them decided to settle in Austin instead of pressing on. With the arrival of women and children came schools and churches. In July 1863, the Methodists established a Sunday

(*Above*) During its heyday, Austin boasted a number of saloons, including this one which is inside the International Hotel. In addition to their principal roles, these establishments served a variety of functions. In Austin, for example, a saloon became a lecture hall for the noted speaker Artemus Ward, who visited Austin in 1864.

(*Opposite*) As this crowd of locals gathered on the porch for the photographer suggests, Austin was proud of the International Hotel, which was originally built in Virgina City—site of the famous Comstock Lode. It was moved by wagon to Austin in the fall of 1862. The photo at right shows the hotel as it appears today.

(Below) St. George's Church was built in 1878, some 12 years after its Episcopal congregation began holding services. Until they had a pastor and a church of their own, the congregants met in the courthouse and worship was led by a layman named D. M. Godwin.

(Opposite) One of the true-life legends in Nevada history was a grocer named Reuel Gridley, who, after losing a bet, carried a sack of flour a mile-and-a-quarter down the canyon and back. The sack was then repeatedly auctioned off until by 1904, when it was displayed at the St. Louis World's Fair, it had raised somewhere between $100,000 to $275,000 for charity.

(Top) The Main Street Firehouse, pictured here, helped protect the community from the kind of conflagrations that plagued most western towns. Austin, which was solidly built, endured relatively few such catastrophes although it did experience a particularly devastating fire in August 1881 at a time when the community's fortunes were already starting to sag.

(Above) This intriguing brick ornamentation comes from a building that replaced one of the frame structures lost in the 1870 fire. Initially it was a bathhouse, then it became a men's clothing store, and today it is the home of True Value Hardware. The motif seen here is fairly common in Austin.

School, the Episcopalians worshiped in the courthouse until they got a church in 1878, and the Catholics dedicated the handsome St. Augustine's in 1866. In time, there were also clubs—including the celebrated Sazerac Lying Club, for those who enjoyed swapping harmless fibs—and public lecture halls. Long before the latter had been built, however, Austin had played host to Artemus Ward, one of the most popular lecturers in the country. After his appearance at one of the local saloons, Ward was attacked by a band of rowdies dressed as Indians and forced at knife-point to repeat his lecture for them. When he reached the climax of his oration, one of the "savages" uttered "Oh, bosh," thereby revealing to the easterner that he'd been had. It was the kind of prank that westerners loved to play on dandies and tenderfeet, but in this case the object of their mirth was not amused.

In 1864, the same year that saw Ward's visit to Austin, the town was incorporated. The ensuing elections, which occurred in April, inspired one of the great stories in the history of the West.

As it happened, a grocer named Reuel Gridley wagered on the outcome of the mayoral election with another Austin citizen, Dr. R. C. Herrick. Grid-

ley's candidate lost and, as a consequence, he was required to carry a sack of flour down the canyon to Clifton. Two days later, with flags waving and a band playing, Gridley marched the mile and a quarter to his destination, his burden on his shoulder and much of the town in his wake. He and his companions refreshed themselves at a Clifton saloon and then proceeded back up the canyon, where the sack of flour was repeatedly auctioned off until it had garnered a total of $4,349 for the Civil War relief fund. As word of the event spread, subsequent auctions of the flour sack were held until finally it and Gridley ended up at the 1904 World's Fair in St. Louis. By then, the legendary foodstuff, which is now on display in the state history museum in Reno, had raised somewhere between $100,000 to $275,000 for charity.

The story of the Gridley flour slack underscores the freewheeling spirit of Austin's early years. Those days came to something of an end, however, in 1865, when the Manhattan Silver

Mining Company consolidated many of the claims in the area and commenced a program of steady ore production that lasted until 1887. In the 1890s, the mines were given new life by J. Phelps Stokes of New York, and at various points in the 20th century, smaller operations have attempted to resurrect production. But by then the community's heyday was long over. Had it not been the seat of Lander County, Austin might well have disappeared like many another once-thriving mining camp. But instead it hung on, occupied by the business of government. Then, in May 1979, voters chose Battle Mountain, which had grown to nearly eight times the size of Austin, as their new county seat.

What will happen to the Old West boom town and its people—about 300 in number—remains to be seen, but for the moment, at least, it offers those with an interest in the lore of the frontier a chance to see the remains of a real live mining town, untouched by the trappings of commercialism.

The Silver State Bar was a lively place indeed when it opened sometime prior to 1870. There were six saloons in Austin at the time and they were all gambling halls. The sorry state of the establishment today can be seen in the color photograph below.

225

(*Above*) At left is the Columbia House restaurant, which stands on the site of one of the town's numerous saloons (the saloon burned down in the 1920s). The building to its left is known today as the Towle and Leavitt Shop. Built in 1857, it had housed a clothing store, an express agency, a drug store, and a saloon.

(*Opposite*) The drug store that was operated on this site by two doctors, G. A. Field and J. McChesney, was destroyed in a fire in 1854. The structure seen in this photo was built two years later.

They were shopkeepers, farmers, and soldiers, dreamers from every place and every walk of life, seeking their fortunes in the land called California. To get there, some of them traveled for months—overland, along dusty trails filled with hazards, natural and otherwise, or on ships traversing the Isthmus of Panama or rounding Cape Hope. When they arrived, some had barely enough money for a pick, a pan, a shovel, and a mule. But they came anyway. An estimated 80,000 arrived in 1849 alone, and from James Marshall's original discovery about 50 miles west of Sacramento, they spread out in all directions, establishing some 500 towns before they were through.

One small band of fortune-seekers was headed by Dr. Thaddeus Hildreth. One evening in late March 1850, after an unsuccessful prospecting trip north, in Calavaras County, they decided to spend the night in a large meadow at the foot of the Sierra Nevada mountains. The next morning, one of the party, John Walker, decided to try to his luck in a nearby gulch. To his surprise, he found what the miners called color. Walker was joined by his companions, the panning proceeded, and in two hours, more than an ounce of gold had been unearthed. What began as a night's stopover became home.

Word of the Hildreth party's discovery soon drew other fortune-seekers and those who followed in their wake—gamblers, saloonkeepers, and prostitutes. By the middle of April, a tent city, which the miners initially called Hildreth's Diggins, had emerged, and in May an official mining district was formed. Along the way, the prospectors chose a more permanent-sounding name for the community— Columbia.

The town's first mayor was Maj. Richard F. Sullivan. In the absence of any other authority, it fell to him to settle disputes between claimholders. One such case concerned a miner named William Smith, who claimed that a Mexican, Juan St. Ann, stole his pair of leather leggings, a useful article of clothing when one is engaged in the rigors of panning for precious metals. After listening to arguments from both sides, Sullivan fined St. Ann three ounces of gold. He then charged Smith one ounce for filing the complaint. The court could not be expected to sit for free, went the mayor's logic. When not playing Solomon, Sullivan found other ways to fill his purse. For instance, he charged a fee to survey and record lots filed by new settlers. Those who refused to pay faced the prospect of losing their claims entirely. Perhaps, in time, the citizens decided that they should not have to pay extor-

It was prospectors like these who initially gave rise to Columbia, California. But, as this photo taken in the Dakotas suggests, water was integral to placer mining and that commodity was in short supply in the Columbia area until the development of aqueducts.

(Above) During the town's heyday, the Wells Fargo Office, built in 1858, was a busy place indeed, for it was here that the miners shipped out their findings. It is estimated that the scales inside the building, which are original to the structure, weighed out about $55 million worth of gold in their day.

(Opposite) The barber shop pictured here opened in 1865, although the town boasted several similar establishments during the previous decade. In the rear of the building are miners' baths. Providing such accommodations was expected of a barber in the mid-19th century.

(Right). The California gold rush began after this man, James Marshall, discovered "color" on the American River, near what is now Sacramento, while building a mill for John A. Sutter.

(Far right) The building that was originally a bakery serves now as a Chinese herb shop and small temple. It reminds visitors to the state park of the contributions made by the Chinese people who came to the United States as contract laborers, in many cases for the railroad. Some of them stayed on and mined their own claims or opened their own businesses.

The wagon pictured here serves as a reminder of the community's struggle against starvation in 1862 when heavy rains and snows made the roads into and out of town virtually impassable and supplies could not get through. The building in the background is the Brady Building, erected in 1899, long after Columbia's heyday had passed.

tion money for law and order, because Sullivan gave up his unique brand of prospecting and moved to nearby Sonora.

Because of the richness of the Columbia find, which was part of the Mother Lode, the relatively small area, and the large influx of miners, the size of each claim was regulated. Moreover, those who were not previous residents of California were taxed $20 a month, and non-whites and foreigners were prohibited from owning claims. These restrictions and a dire lack of water, which severely hindered the men's ability to prospect, quickly reduced the population from about 1,000 in May 1850 to a mere hundred by June. When the rains came in November, however, the miners returned.

Clearly a reliable source of water was needed. In June 1851, the Tuolumne County Water Company was formed to divert water to the mines from the nearby Stanislaus River, and any miner who worked on the ditch was to receive a share of stock in the enterprise and $5 a day.

Meanwhile, the miners' tax had been relaxed, and Columbia started taking on the trappings of a more permanent community. By November 1851 a significant number of buildings were under construction, some made of logs, others of board which had been cut at the new sawmill. The first newspaper, the *Columbia Star*, premiered in October. It lasted only a few issues, but it was succeeded by the *Columbia Gazette* the following month.

Town growth was further enhanced by the completion of the first aqueduct in May 1852. Even though it was insufficient for the miners' needs, confidence in Columbia's future was high. July even saw the construction of two churches, and several private schools were in session before year's end. The opening of such institutions meant that families were beginning to establish themselves among the typically free-spirited prospectors. The women and children could patronize some 150 businesses, including four banks, seven bakeries, two book and stationery stores, and three meat markets. There was even a post office and a theater, and in 1853, the town's first brick building was constructed.

Finally, in December 1852, the Tuolumne County Water Company completed its second aqueduct, which was billed as the longest canal in the state, "supplying water to (the) most valuable placer diggins in California."

Like all frontier towns, Columbia experienced hardships on its way toward stability. In late 1852, for example, the town was struck by a smallpox epidemic, which resulted in considerable loss of life. That year also brought heavy rains and snows that made the roads into and out of town virtually impassable. The isolated town experienced a severe shortage of provisions and had to pay extremely high prices for those that made it through. By April 1853, however, the roads became passable again, ample supplies began arriving, and the prices declined.

Meanwhile another source of conflict had surfaced—the high cost of water. When the miners' request for a price reduction failed to move the Tuolumne County Water Company, the residents began to consider alternatives. Finally in 1854 they formed the

(Right) Engaging frontier graphics highlight the entrance to the home of Tuolumne Engine Co. No. 1. Inside one can find Papeete, a two-cylinder fire engine manufactured in 1852 by Hunneman and Company of Boston. The locals were justly proud of their acquisition. As seen in the photo above, a photographer captured a group of them posing with the hand-pumper.

Fire was the bane of every frontier community, and Columbia was no exception, having experienced devastating blazes in 1854 and again in 1857. The firehouse pictured here stands on the site of what was once the home of Columbia Engine Co. No. 2.

(Left) Seen here is the parlor of the City Hotel, begun in 1857. The two-story structure, which includes 20 bedrooms, was one of the largest buildings in town during Columbia's heyday. Restored in 1974, it once again serves as a guest house, operated by students in resort management at the nearby junior college.

(Below) In many cases in the West, including that of the Columbia drug store seen here, a physician was also a druggist, mixing remedies himself from bottled ingredients and herbs that he grew in his own backyard. Patent medicines, such as Dr. John Bull's Vegetable Worm Destroyer, were the staples of any frontier pharmacy. Of course, they were little more than hard liquor, but few complained about that.

Columbia and Stanislaus River Water Company, and set out to build a 60-mile aqueduct for their own use.

When they weren't talking about water, the folks in Columbia were probably discussing the murder of Capt. John Parrot, which took place in November 1853. It seems that Parrot had been drinking in a saloon when he was assaulted with a knife by a drunken Austrian named Peter Nicholas. He died from his wounds shortly therafter.

After nearly being lynched by a mob of vigilantes, Nicholas was tried, found guilty of murder, and sentenced to death. By an odd twist of fate, however, he ended up serving only seven years in prison. Legend has it that, at the time the state's governor was considering Nicholas' case, he received a petition signed by 10,000 Columbia citizens. It concerned the prospect of making the town the state capital, but somehow the nature of the request was replaced by one asking for clemency for the Austrian. Moved by the wishes of so many voters, the state's chief executive acquiesced.

The telegraph arrived in Columbia in 1854, but one month earlier the community's forward momentum had been slowed by a major fire which virtually destroyed the entire business district. Many of the structures that replaced them were made of brick, to prevent a recurrence of the disaster. In addition, fire hydrants were placed in strategic locations around town, and a 44-gallon water reservoir was constructed. Nevertheless, August 1857 brought another inferno. This time, when Columbia rebuilt, every building had to be freestanding. Moreover, merchants were expected to keep on hand three buckets and two barrels of water. The community's reconstruction was also accompanied by the installation of 15 street lights. When they were turned on in January 1858, Columbia became the first town in California to have gas lighting. That same year brought an even more important project to fruition—the Columbia and Stanislaus River Water Company's ditch. It insured that the miners would have an adequate water supply even in years of drought.

Despite these inroads, prospectors in Columbia had little to celebrate in 1858. Most of the gold that could be found through the method known as placer mining was gone. It would take companies, not individuals, and hydraulic mining, not a pick, a pan, or a sluice box, to extract whatever precious minerals remained. Many of the fortune-seekers began drifting off to new finds and new hopes.

The town's decline was furthered by the heavy rains of 1862, which produced 102 inches of precipitation. In a repeat of what had happened 10 years earlier, Columbia was virtually cut off from the outside world and many residents were near starvation before the flooding ended.

Finally Columbia began turning inward. As individual buildings fell vacant, they were razed and the lots became the basis of new mining activity. But, by 1868, even these sites were about played out. The population, which had reached perhaps as high as 6,000 in the town's heyday, had dropped to 500, and the last newspaper in town, the *Columbia City Citizen News*, went out of business.

In 1945 the State of California seized the opportunity to preserve what remained of the town, creating the Columbia State Historic Park. The result today includes 44 restored or re-created structures, ranging from the Fallon Hotel/Theater, which still offers live performances, to the Miners' Supply store, where visitors can purchase pans and try their own luck at the diggings.

(Left) In 1860 the construction of a two-story, brick school-house commenced on Cemetery Hill. When classes started the following year the furniture that the ladies' committee had ordered had not yet arrived so the students had to make do temporarily with what was on hand. The structure remained operational until 1937 and was restored in 1960.

(Below) Situated in the heart of the Mother Lode country, Columbia yielded up some $87 million worth of gold during its 20 years as an active mining community. Visitors to the state historic park today can try their luck at the diggings, with equipment available for purchase at the Matelot Gulch Miners' Supply.

(Above) The Larkin House is a good example of the Monterey Colonial style, which combines features of New England architecture, including a hip roof, central hall, and interior stairway, with such Mexican elements as adobe walls, second-floor balcony with overhanging roof, and a walled garden.

(Opposite) The revenues that were collected at the Custom House in Monterey Bay provided the primary source of income for the Mexican colonial government between 1822 and 1846. On view in the facility today are wares typical of an 1830s merchant ship.

It is hard to imagine the U.S. army taking a city from a foreign power at gunpoint and then meekly returning its new acquisition the following day. But in 1842 that is what happened in Monterey, California.

At the time, American naval forces in the West were under orders to occupy the ports of California—then part of Mexico—if war erupted between the United States and its neighbor to the south. In September of that year, Comm. Thomas ap Catesby Jones, the commander of America's Pacific fleet, received a communication that led him to believe that indeed the two nations were embattled.

Jones immediately sailed north from Peru, where he was at anchor. Upon reaching Monterey Bay on October 19, 1842, he demanded that the governor surrender the town and its military forces, which the governor did the following day. Thereafter, the Stars and Stripes were raised above the military outpost that overlooked the harbor. The whole affair had been handled neatly, efficiently, and without bloodshed.

There was only one problem, as Jones discovered when he came ashore and examined several recent newspapers.

(Right) This house, which dates from 1840, was home to Robert Louis Stevenson for three months in 1879. The celebrated British writer came to Monterey to be near Fanny Osbourne, a married woman with whom he fell in love. Eventually Fanny divorced her husband and married the author of *Treasure Island*.

(Below) This bedroom in the Larkin House is indicative of the high style in which the successful merchant, Thomas Oliver Larkin, and his family lived. A native of Massachusetts, Larkin settled in Monterey in 1832, married a widow who was also from Massachusetts, and became a wealthy landholder, as well as U.S. consul to California.

The United States and Mexico were not at war. He had taken the capital city of a foreign power without provocation. Under the circumstances, he did the only things he could do. He restored the Mexican flag to its place over the fort and apologized for his actions to the governor and citizens of the community.

The town that the Californios reclaimed had been founded 72 years before Jones' arrival, when Capt. Gaspar de Portolá and Father Junipero Serra of Spain established a fortress and mission on Monterey Bay as part of King Charles III's plan to bolster his empire against reported incursions by Russia. The inlet had been discovered in 1602 by explorer Sebastián Vizcáino, who named it in honor of the viceroy of New Spain, the Count of Monterey.

Fulfilling his assignment did not come easily to Portolá. More than half his complement of 300 men died on the journey north from Baja California. Moreover, when the survivors reached the area they did not recognize it from Vizcáino's description. In fact, they continued north, discovered San Francisco Bay, which had apparently eluded previous explorers, returned to Monterey Bay, again did not recognize it, and continued south to San Diego. It was only in San Diego that Portolá realized his mistake. After waiting out the winter in the south, Portolá again set out for Monterey Bay, with Father Serra and another party of soldiers following by sea. This time they met with success and the mission and presidio were officially founded on June 3, 1770.

While Portolá occupied himself with military and political matters, Serra began converting the 800 or so Rumsens who inhabited the area. The Indians, who were members of the Ohlone tribe, were willing to be baptized, but they didn't realize that thereafter the Spanish would virtually imprison them to insure their adherence to the tenets of their new faith. Not only did the Rumsens lose their traditional way of life, but also many died from exposure to diseases—measles, smallpox, diph-

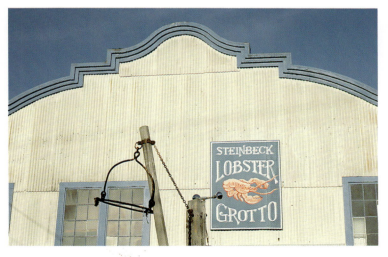

(Above) In 1848, after San Jose became the capital of California, Monterey lost much of its population to the gold rush and to the burgeoning city of San Francisco. By the 1870s, it was a village of some 400 and fishing and agriculture were the principal sources of income.

(Above) When many people think of Monterey today, they think of Cannery Row and the novels of the Nobel Prize-winning author, John Steinbeck. The Steinbeck Lobster Grotto, pictured here, is a product of one and named for the other.

(Left) In 1770, Capt. Gaspar de Portolá, pictured here, and Father Junipero Serra established a fortress and mission on Monterey Bay as part of Spanish monarch Charles III's plan to bolster his empire against reported incursions by Russia. The town of Monterey grew from there.

by Richard Henry Dana in his book *Two Years Before the Mast*.

Eleven years after the author's visit and four years after Commodore Jones' aborted conquest of Monterey, another American sailor arrived in town. His name was John Drake Sloat and, like Jones, he was commander of the U.S. naval forces in the Pacific. Also like Jones he was under orders to secure the ports of California for his country. But this time America and Mexico really were at war with one another.

Sloat arrived in Monterey Bay on July 2, 1846, almost two months after the outbreak of hostilities. Still, the 68-year-old commander, remembering his predecessor's impetuosity, proceeded with caution. Rather than demand the town's surrender or threaten force, he and Thomas Larkin, by then the American consul, authored a rather remarkable proclamation, which the Commodore issued on July 6. It promised the local citizens that as part of the United States they would "enjoy the same rights and privileges they now enjoy; together with the privilege of choosing their own magistrates and other officers for the administration of justice among themselves; and the same protection will be extended to them as to any other state in the Union." On the following day, the military commandant of Monterey handed over the town.

Within weeks of Monterey's accession to the United States, Walter Colton was appointed the new mayor. The energetic, judicious Yale graduate soon founded California's first newspaper, the *Californian*, impaneled the first American jury on the West Coast, and erected the territory's first schoolhouse and meeting place, which became known as Colton Hall.

With the end of the Mexican War on February 2, 1848, Colton hoped for California's orderly transition from Mexican to American rule. But the gold rush intervened and the influx of 50,000 fortune seekers over the next two years brought chaos instead. Finally, in September 1849, a constitutional convention for the proposed

(Above) Colton Hall was erected in 1848/49 at the behest of Monterey's first American mayor, Walter Colton, pictured at left. Seen here is the second floor of the school-house–public meeting hall, which has been restored to its appearance in September 1849, when the California constitution was drafted here.

theria—for which they had no immunity. Still, Serra's successful efforts gave rise to several more missions and, in 1775, Monterey became the capital of Alta California. After Mexico gained its independence in 1821, Californios, who were part of the new nation, suddenly found themselves free to trade with foreign powers—notably the United States, Great Britain, and Russia—whose ships regularly plied the Pacific coast. Under Spain, such commerce had been illegal, although the prohibition had frequently been ignored.

The opening of trade to foreigners brought a number of Yankee settlers to the area, among them Capt. John R. Cooper, who became a successful Monterey merchant, along with his half-brother, Thomas Oliver Larkin. The Mexican government welcomed the newcomers, providing they converted to Catholicism. Some took Spanish names—Cooper, for example, became Juan Bautista Cooper—and married into locally prominent families.

The late 1820s and 1830s brought considerable growth to Monterey, described as "the pleasantest and most civilized-looking place in California" state of California was held in Colton Hall. The result was a document that, among other things, called for the abolition of slavery. When the issue of California statehood came before the U.S. Congress, this provision sparked tremendous debate among the legislators seeking to preserve the Union's precious balance between slave and free states. Sparked by Senator Henry Clay, the famous Compromise of 1850 was reached, whereby California was to be admitted into the Union as a free state and the other lands acquired from Mexico would be organized into territories without restrictions on slavery.

Another provision in the California constitution had dramatic consequences for Monterey. It called for the relocation of the capital to San Jose. With the passage of this document, the venerable city's leadership role in California government came to an end.

By the latter part of the 19th century, Monterey had become a village of some 400 residents, including many Portuguese whalers, and fishing and agriculture were the mainstays of the economy. Renewed life came early in the 20th century as a small, locally prolific fish made Monterey the Sardine Capital of the World. At one point as many as nine canneries were processing some 1.4 million cases of sardines per year. In the early 1950s, the local pool of sardines was exhausted and the flourishing industry died, but the memory of those halcyon days live on in the books of Nobel Prize-winning novelist, John Steinbeck.

Today, tourism is Monterey's biggest source of income, as people come to the area to enjoy its scenic beauty; to partake of the town's many annual cultural events, including the celebrated Monterey Jazz Festival; and to tour more than 50 historic buildings. Among them are several restored residences; the Custom House, which provided the colonial Mexican government with its principal source of income between 1822 and 1846; and Colton Hall, where the California state constitution was drafted.

(Above) Completed in 1795, the stone-and-adobe Mission of San Carlos Borromeo replaced an earlier adobe structure that was destroyed by fire in 1789. The bell tower and other elements were added later, but much of the present structure is original.

(Below) The parlor of the Cooper-Molera House has been restored to reflect the life of an upper-class Californio household in the middle of the 19th century. The original owner, John Rogers Cooper, changed his name to Juan Bautista Cooper and married a member of the aristocratic Vallejo family.

(Above) John Drake Sloat was commander of America's naval forces in the Pacific in 1846, when hostilities erupted between Mexico and the United States. With the help of Thomas Larkin, he was able to secure Monterey for the U.S. without firing a shot.

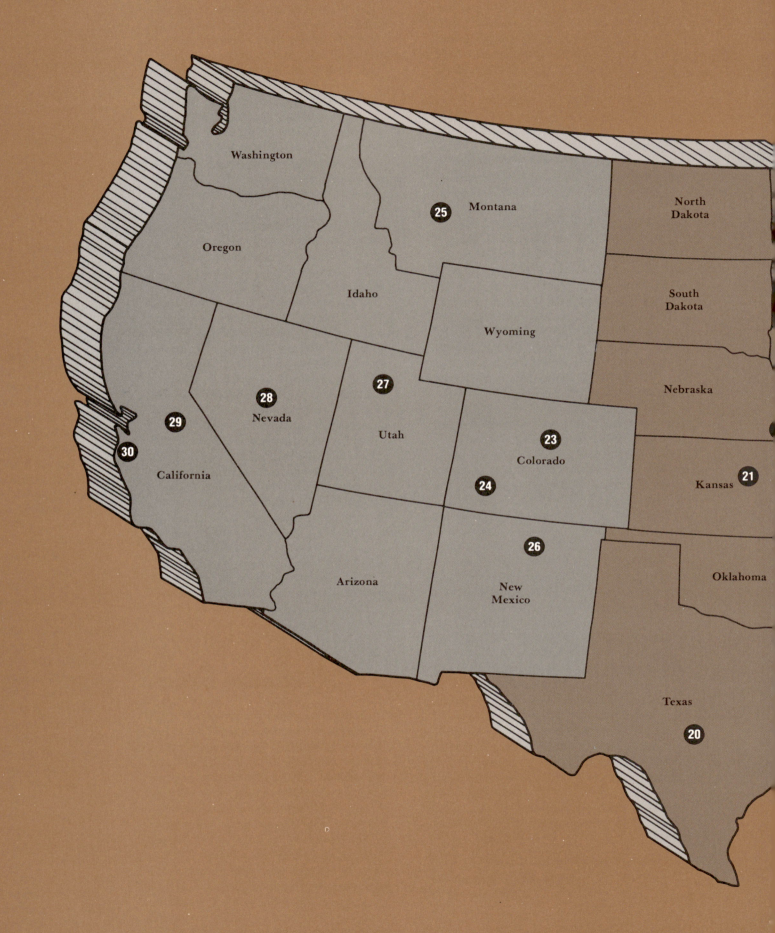